USS Lexington CV-2

Written by David Doyle

Squadron At Sea®

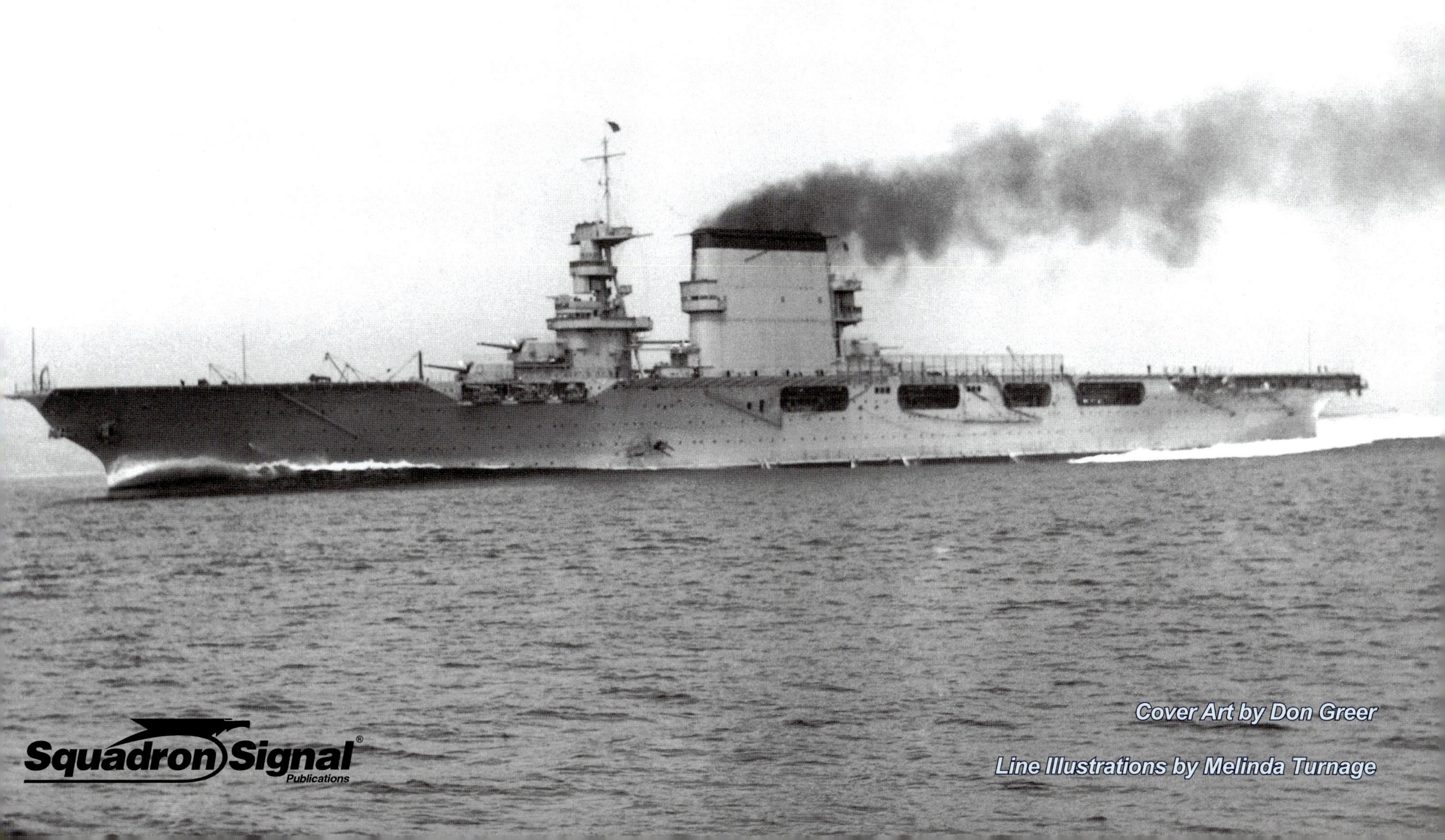

Cover Art by Don Greer

Line Illustrations by Melinda Turnage

Squadron/Signal® Publications

(FRONT COVER) *Lexington* entered service during the "yellow wing" era of U.S. Naval aviation, when carrier decks swarmed with shining, silver-doped, fabric-covered aircraft adorned with chrome yellow wing tops. *Lexington* and her sister ship *Saratoga* would be the world's largest aircraft carriers until 1944.

(BACK COVER) What began as moderate damage incurred during the Battle of the Coral Sea in May 1942 turned catastrophic when aviation gasoline vapors ignited and set off a series of fires and ordnance explosions that tore through Lady Lex. The ship was abandoned and ultimately scuttled, becoming the U.S. Navy's most serious loss in an engagement that nevertheless marked a strategic victory over the Japanese.

2

About the Squadron At Sea Series®

The *Squadron At Sea* series details a specific ship using color and black-and-white archival photographs and photographs of in-service, preserved, and restored equipment. *Squadron At Sea* titles are devoted to civilian and military vessels, while *On Deck*® titles are devoted to warships. These picture books focus on specific vessels from the laying of the keel to present or its finale.

 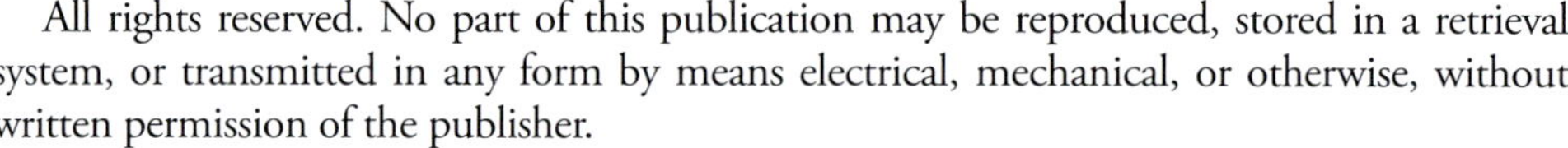

Proudly printed in the U.S.A.
Copyright 2013 Squadron/Signal Publications
1115 Crowley Drive, Carrollton, TX 75006-1312 U.S.A.

Hard Cover ISBN 978-0-89747-714-7
Soft Cover ISBN 978-0-89747-715-4

Military/Combat Photographs and Snapshots

If you have any photos of aircraft, armor, soldiers, or ships of any nation, particularly wartime snapshots, please share them with us and help make Squadron/Signal's books all the more interesting and complete in the future. Any photograph sent to us will be copied and returned. Electronic images are preferred. The donor will be fully credited for any photos used. Please send them to:

Squadron/Signal Publications
1115 Crowley Drive
Carrollton, TX 75006-1312 U.S.A.
www.SquadronSignalPublications.com

(TITLE PAGE) The USS *Lexington* – affectionately referred to as "Lady Lex" – was the United States Navy's second aircraft carrier. Laid down as the lead ship of the *Lexington*-class battlecruisers, which were to have been the world's most powerful warships, the Washington Naval Treaty forbade her completion as such, although permitting her to be finished as an aircraft carrier. She is shown here, her turbo-electric drive making speed, as smoke billows from her funnel, which sports an identifying band of black paint around its top.

Dedication

To the families of the 216 patriots who steamed out of Pearl Harbor on 15 April 1942, and like their ship, did not come home.

Introduction

When the keel of the *Lexington* was laid on the ways of the Fore River Ship and Engine Building Company, Quincy, Massachusetts, on 8 January 1921 she was the lead ship of what was to be the most powerful class of battlecruisers in the world. The new battlecruiser class, authorized by the Naval Act of 1916, was to include six ships – *Lexington, Constellation, Saratoga, Ranger, Constitution,* and *United States.* Authorized at the same time were six *South Dakota* (BB-49)-class battleships, which together with battlecruisers would make the U.S. Navy perhaps the single most powerful fleet in the world. Coincidentally, when in 1919 Naval aviators were pushing for a newly constructed specialized aircraft carrier, the Navy's first, this was denied, citing the strained budget caused by the ambitious 1916 battleship/battlecruiser building program.

Originally each of the battlecruisers was to be armed with ten 14-inch, 50-caliber rifles, but by the time construction of the ships had begun, the intended armament had been changed to eight 16-inch, 50-caliber rifles. In terms of naval weaponry, the caliber of the gun is the barrel length divided by the bore – thus a 16-inch, 50-caliber gun is 800 inches long. Battlecruiser design theory was to create a very heavily armed, relatively lightly armored, warship, which relied upon unusually high speed as a key element of its defense. The *Lexington* was designed to steam at 35-knots, a pace unheard of at the time for such a large vessel. To attain this speed required a whopping 180,000 horsepower, six times more powerful than the largest machinery the U.S. Navy had built up to that time, the 29,000 horsepower *West Virginia* (BB-48). The *Lexingtons* were to displace 43,500 tons each, making them the heaviest ships in the fleet.

All these ambitious projects were cast into disarray with the signing of the Washington Naval Treaty on 6 February 1922. That international agreement, by means of which the United States hoped to promote general disarmament and particularly curtail Japan's rapid naval expansion, required the immediate suspension of capital ship construction by all signatory countries. For the United States, it spelled the end of the Navy's battlecruiser plans. The treaty did, however, permit each signatory to use two existing capital ship hulls as the basis for aircraft carriers with a displacement not to exceed 33,000 tons each (versus the 27,000-ton limit otherwise imposed on carriers). *Lexington,* CC-1, under construction at Fore River Shipyard, Quincy, Massachusetts, and *Saratoga,* CC-3, being built by New York Shipbuilding, Camden, New Jersey, were 24.2 percent and 28 percent complete, respectively, when construction was suspended in February 1922. As the two battlecruisers closest to completion, they were selected for conversion to aircraft carriers. The rest of the class, which ranged in completion from 22.7 percent for the *Constellation* to 4 percent for *Ranger,* were scrapped on the builders' ways.

Concurrently with the treaty negotiations, the Navy had been exploring an assortment of new aircraft carrier designs, ever-hopeful that funds would be released to build an aircraft carrier. Among these hypothetical designs was one with a projected displacement of 39,000 tons and a length of 850 feet, whose preliminary design was delivered 5 May 1921. When the treaty was signed, it took only until 17 February 1922 to adapt the 1921 design to the *Lexington*-class hull. However, largely to meet the treaty-imposed weight limitations, this design required further refinement, and it was 21 December 1923 before final plans were approved and the yards were instructed to proceed with the conversion of the two vessels, retaining their names but changing their hull numbers to CV-2 and CV-3.

After delays in construction, primarily due to continued haggling over the weight limit, *Lexington* was finally launched on 3 October 1925. She was christened by Mrs. Theodore Douglas Robinson, whose husband was the Assistant Secretary of the Navy. Though in the water, *Lexington* was still far from being ready to put to sea. Tugs pushed her immense, powerless hull along the Weymouth Fore River to the shipyard's fitting pier. There she was moored for the next two years as a bevy of workers transformed the hulk into a state-of the-art aircraft carrier. Finally completed, she was commissioned on 14 December 1927, at last getting the coveted "USS" before her name. Captain Albert W. Marshall was placed in command that day, becoming the first of what would be 10 officers who would command *Lexington.*

After her commissioning, *Lexington* moved to Charleston Navy Yard in South Boston on 5 January 1925 for final fitting out. *En route,* Captain Marshall took her into Massachusetts Bay just long enough for a Vought UO-1 to land aboard. This was the first landing aboard a *Lexington*-class carrier, beating the previously-launched *Saratoga* by about a week. After fitting out, *Lexington* set out on her shakedown cruise along the U.S. East Coast. *Lexington* sailed west through the Panama Canal, bound for the U.S. West Coast, where she would be based from her 7 April 1928 arrival in San Pedro until her eventual loss.

Acknowledgments

Warships, particularly capital ships, touch many lives. Their complexity, long service life, and considerable range bring them into contact with many more people than does, for example, a single tank or specific airplane. Accordingly, archival resources concerning the *Lexington* were scattered from coast to coast and through the collections of a multitude of individuals and institutions, many which generously opened their resources for the creation of this book.

I would like to thank fellow authors Tom Kailbourn, Robert C. Stern, A.D. Baker III, and Scott Taylor for their help with this project. Researchers Tracy White, Martin Quinn, Jerry Leslie, Roger Torgeson, Rick Davis, and Patty and James Noblin were very generous in sharing their discoveries with me. The archival resources of the National Archives at College Park, Maryland; San Bruno, California; and Seattle, Washington, yielded many treasures of information, as did the Hawaii State Archives, National Museum of Naval Aviation, San Diego Air and Space Museum, Puget Sound Naval Shipyard, the U.S. Naval Shipbuilding Museum, the Naval Historical Foundation, various branches of the National Park Service, and the U.S. Army Museum of Hawaii. Robert Hanshew, Lisa Crunk, and Chuck Haberlein at the Naval History and Heritage Command were generous with their time and providing access to the collection to complete this study.

The dedicated staff at Squadron Signal Publications have invested long hours in reviving worn and faded photographs, and ensuring that my words not only are accurate, but are also clear. My wonderful wife Denise scanned hundreds of images and sifted through thousands of pages of dusty documents helping to pull together the materials presented here.

All photos not otherwise credited are from the collection of the U.S. National Archives and Records Administration, College Park, Maryland.

An artist's conception depicts *Lexington* as she would have looked if she had been completed as a battlecruiser. Of the six ships originally planned for the *Lexington*-class battlecruisers, only two, *Lexington* and *Saratoga,* were completed, but during their construction they were converted to aircraft carriers. The remaining vessels of the class, although begun, were scrapped on the builders' ways.

The rise of Japan in the years after World War I led many U.S. policy makers to believe that the next major war would take place in the Pacific. To prepare strategies and men for such an eventuality, the Navy conducted numerous exercises in that ocean during the interwar years. *Lexington's* debut in such training came in a January 1929 scenario dubbed Fleet Problem IX, wherein *Lexington* was assigned to the Blue Force, tasked with defending the Panama Canal from the Black Force, which included her sister ship *Saratoga.* Prior to this exercise, carriers – specifically the *Langley,* the sole U.S. carrier in earlier years – had played only minor scouting roles. With Fleet Problem IX, however, the judges not only determined that the mock attack by *Saratoga's* aircraft had "destroyed" one end of the canal, but that during the course of the drill each carrier's aircraft had "badly damaged" if not "sunk" the opposing force's carrier. Carriers would play more central roles in future exercises and *Lexington* and *Saratoga* would face off against each other, and also work together, in many fleet maneuvers until 1941.

It had been planned that the aircraft on *Lexington* would be divided into two fighter (VF) squadrons consisting of 18 operational and nine reserve aircraft each, two torpedo (VT) squadrons comprising 16 operating and eight reserve aircraft each, and half of an observation (VO) squadron of 12 operating and six reserve aircraft. Three additional VO aircraft were assigned to a utility squadron. By the time *Lexington* joined the operational fleet, the squadron designations and assignments had been modified. When she steamed for Panama and Fleet Problem IX, she was carrying Squadrons VF-3B, flying Boeing F3B-1 fighters; VT-1B, flying Martin T4M-1 aircraft; bombing squadron VB-1B, with a mixture of Curtiss F6C-2/3 and Boeing F3B-1 aircraft; and scouting squadron VS-3B, flying Vought O2U-2 airplanes. The "B" suffix on the squadron numbers signified *Lexington's* assignment to the Battle Fleet.

Lexington's captain during Fleet Problem IX was Captain Frank D. Berrien, who had relieved Captain Albert Marshall on 11 August 1928. Captain Berrien was, in turn, relieved on 30 June 1930 by Captain Ernest King, who remained her captain until 31 May 1932. Assigned to radio communications aboard *Lexington* during this time was a 1929 Annapolis graduate, Robert A. Heinlein, whose future writings were influenced by his Navy experiences.

Lexington **was built at the Fore River Plant of Bethlehem Shipbuilding Corp. along the Weymouth Fore River at Quincy, Massachusetts. Originally designated CC-1, her keel was laid on 8 January 1921. In this 29 March 1921 photo, the keel and framing for the double bottom are in place amidships. Plates of the shell, the outer skin of the hull, have been installed on the frame, with some of the shell plates extending beyond the frame.**

By 30 June 1921, the keel and frame of the double bottom have been extended forward but not all the way to the bow. A lateral bulkhead has been erected at the forward end of the ship's vital machinery spaces; three temporary ladders are leaning against the top of the bulkhead. Staging, or scaffolding, rises on each side of the building ways; planks were laid higher and higher on the beams of the scaffolding as the sides of the hull took shape.

The progress of construction of *Lexington* is viewed from off the starboard stern in a 1 October 1921 photograph. The space enclosed by the first two lateral bulkheads will be the location of the main driving motors for the two inboard propellers. Immediately forward of this space, toward the center of the photo, will be ammunition magazines and handling rooms, while on each side will be the main driving motors for the outboard propellers.

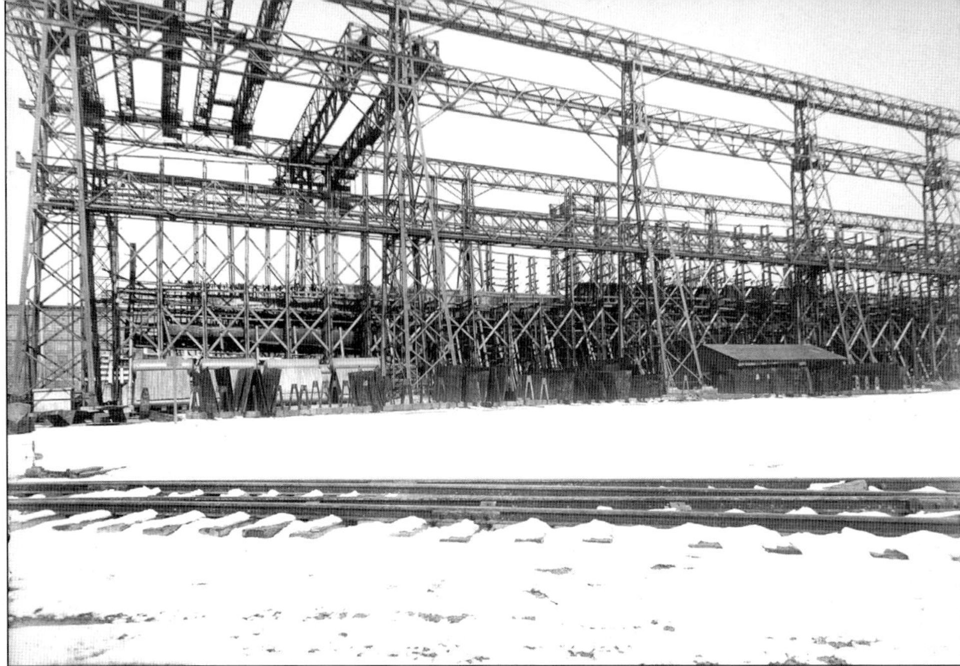

The shape of the *Lexington* as viewed off her port bow is visible behind the staging and crane supports in a 1 March 1922 photo. Unlike her sister ship, *Saratoga*, which was built under a massive shed at Camden, New Jersey, *Lexington* was built out in the open.

Rather than scrap *Lexington* and *Saratoga* under terms of the Washington Naval Treaty, the Navy drafted plans to convert them to aircraft carriers. In March 1922 a panel of admirals uses models to explain the conversion to the House Naval Affairs Committee. (National Museum of Naval Aviation)

The *Lexington* is viewed from amidships toward the bow on 14 February 1922. Snow blankets the deck plates in the foreground, while the beams that will support the deck as it is extended forward are visible in the background. During the month this photo was taken, construction on the *Lexington* was suspended under the strictures of the Washington Naval Treaty; the ship was 24.2 percent complete.

The barbettes for the four twin 16-inch turrets of the *Lexington* are under construction on 1 March 1922. If the ship had been completed as a battlecruiser, the barbettes would have held operating machinery and ammunition-handling spaces below the turrets.

On 1 July 1922 authorization was approved to complete *Lexington* and *Saratoga* as aircraft carriers. On 3 October 1922, the progress of work on Airplane Carrier No. 2, as *Lexington* had been redesignated, is seen from over the forward part of the hull.

Lexington is viewed facing aft on 17 January 1923. The shell has been extended one strake, or horizontal course of plates, above the deck in the foreground. The frame of the ship was built up in sections. In the background, the stern has not yet been built up to the level of the deck in the foreground. Below the level of the third deck from frame 173 to the stern was an armored platform that protected the steering gear.

The area of the ship in the background of the preceding photo is viewed close-up on 17 January 1923. On the *Lexington*-class carriers, the third deck (i.e., the third full deck below the flight deck) was the armored deck, comprising a layer of 50-pound STS (special treatment steel) over one of 30-pound STS, yielding a thickness of two inches. Armored flight decks were not introduced on U.S. carriers until after World War II.

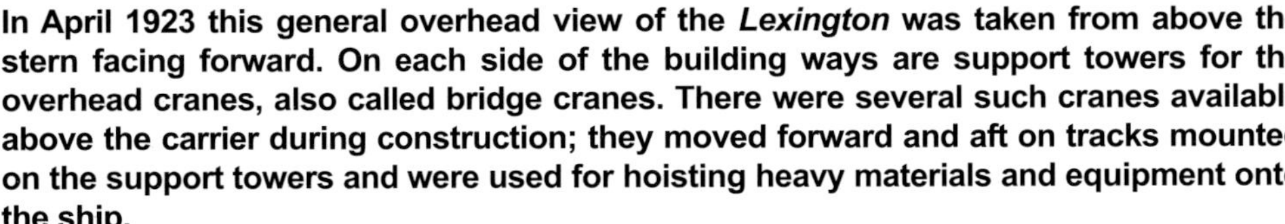

In April 1923 this general overhead view of the *Lexington* was taken from above the stern facing forward. On each side of the building ways are support towers for the overhead cranes, also called bridge cranes. There were several such cranes available above the carrier during construction; they moved forward and aft on tracks mounted on the support towers and were used for hoisting heavy materials and equipment onto the ship.

The photographer was positioned over frame 193 well aft on the *Lexington*, probably poised on an overhead crane, when he took this photo facing forward to document the state of construction on 12 July 1923. Farther forward, amidships, work is underway on a transverse bulkhead and some of the compartments on the outboard sides of the deck. In the background toward the bow, much of the plating of this deck remains to be installed.

This elevated view of the *Lexington* was taken from above frame 104 facing aft on 24 January 1924. At the center of the photo, work has begun on a deck, apparently the main deck, with the structure of the aft elevator well taking shape on that piece of deck. To the right, the indentation in the deck with the curve at its aft end is the floor and lower part of a boat pocket, one of four such pockets built into the port side of the hull to house boats.

Work on the hangar deck, or second deck, is documented in an 11 April 1924 photo taken above frame 104 facing forward. Much of the hangar deck would be occupied by hangar space, where spare aircraft and those requiring maintenance would be housed. This deck would also hold crew quarters, the laundry, stowage spaces, vegetable lockers, ventilation ducts, the boiler uptakes, CPO mess rooms, the sick bay, and other compartments.

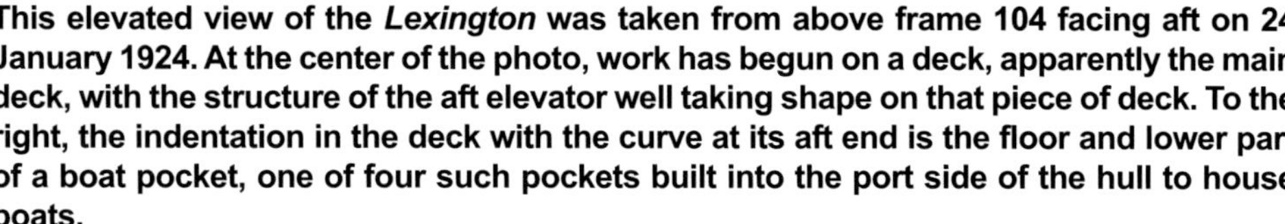

In a view taken above frame 82 facing toward the bow on 14 October 1924, in the foreground is the partially completed flight deck and the forward elevator well, which would be T-shaped once the flight deck was extended forward of the well.

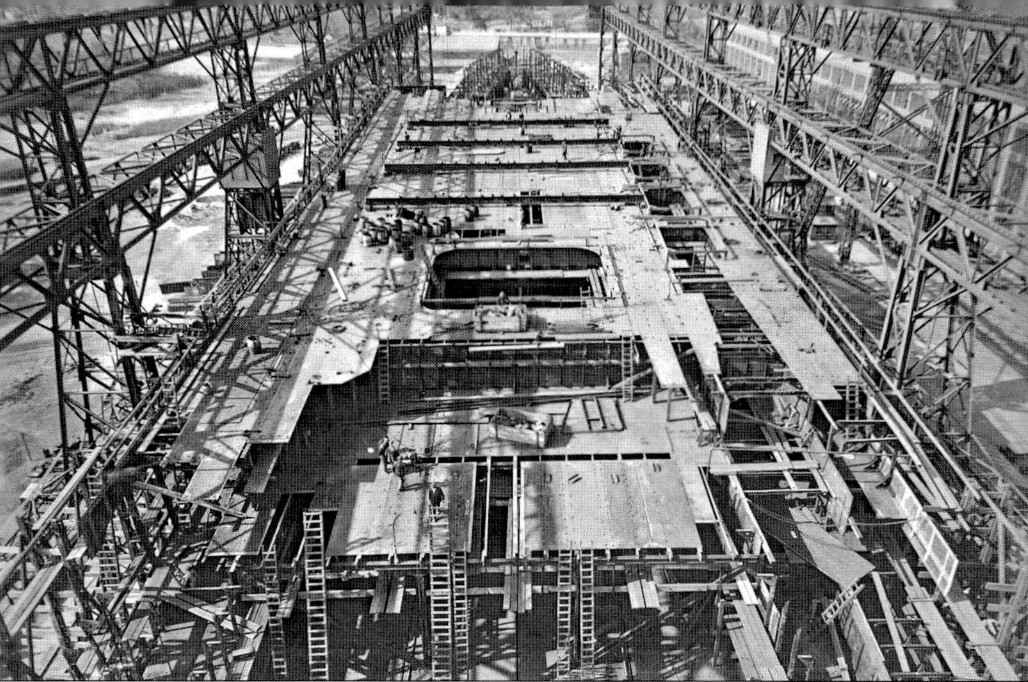

In another 14 October 1924 photo, the *Lexington* is viewed from above frame 133 facing forward. The uppermost deck is the flight deck, and it is pierced by the rectangular aft elevator well. Below the flight deck are the uncompleted main and hangar decks.

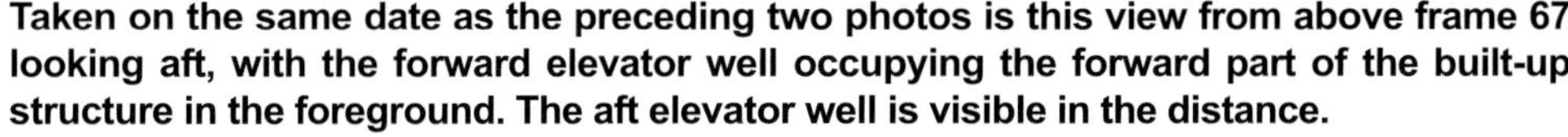

Taken on the same date as the preceding two photos is this view from above frame 67 looking aft, with the forward elevator well occupying the forward part of the built-up structure in the foreground. The aft elevator well is visible in the distance.

As seen facing aft from frame 127 on 15 January 1925, the aft part of the hull of the *Lexington* was slowly being built upwards after the amidships area had been built as far upward as the flight deck. Compartments are under construction to the sides.

The flight deck of the *Lexington* is observed from frame 130 forward on 23 April 1925. The aft elevator well is in the foreground. The four rectangular openings in the flight deck to the right are boiler uptakes, which will be routed up through the smokestack.

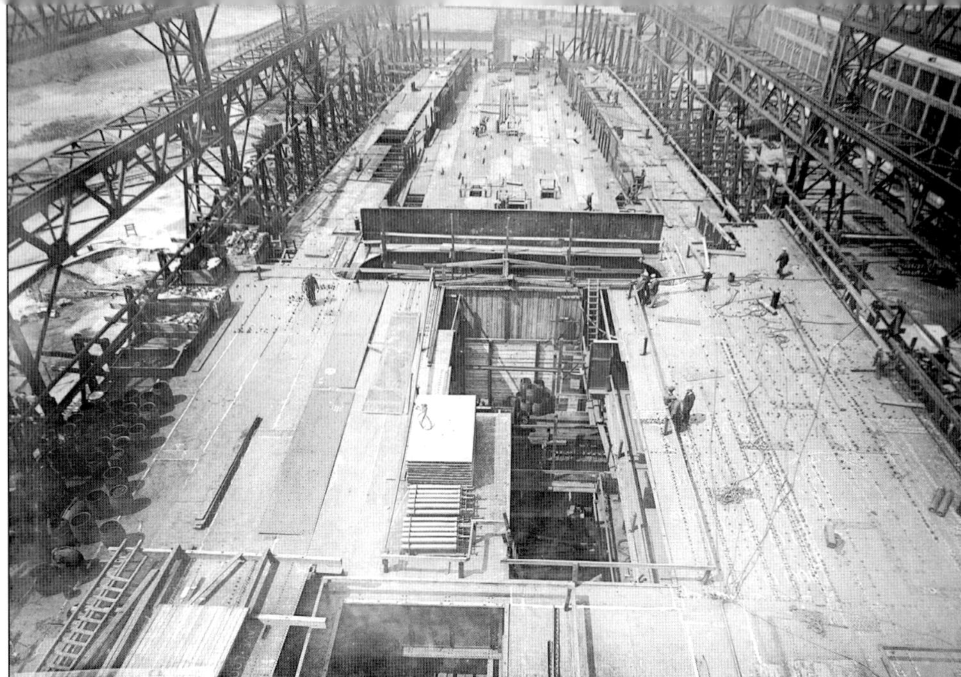

Also taken on 23 April 1925, this view shows the flight deck facing forward from frame 92. Work on the flight deck had proceeded only to the front of the forward elevator; forward of that point, work continues on the lower decks toward the bow.

The rudder of the *Lexington* is seen from the starboard side on 23 April 1925. Several scaffold planks are set up next to the front edge of the rudder. Also in view above the scaffolding to the right is the starboard inboard propeller bracket, or propeller strut.

By 10 July 1925, the propellers and propeller shafts had been fitted to the *Lexington*. The rudder is turned hard to starboard. The design of the stern is also displayed. The rear of the ramp at the aft end of the flight deck came even with the top of the stern.

The *Lexington* was photographed on the building ways at Fore River on 2 October 1925, the day before her launching. Scaffolding has been cleared from the area, leaving only the overhead cranes and their support towers standing. Light-colored poppets attached to the bottom of the hull will stabilize and protect the narrow forward part of the hull during launching. On the upper part of the side of the hull, the forward gun gallery and the four boat pockets are visible.

On the day before her launching, a photographer on an overhead crane took this view of the forward part of the flight deck, with the forward elevator at the bottom of the photo. The round opening in the deck to the right is for mounting the forward 8-inch gun turret.

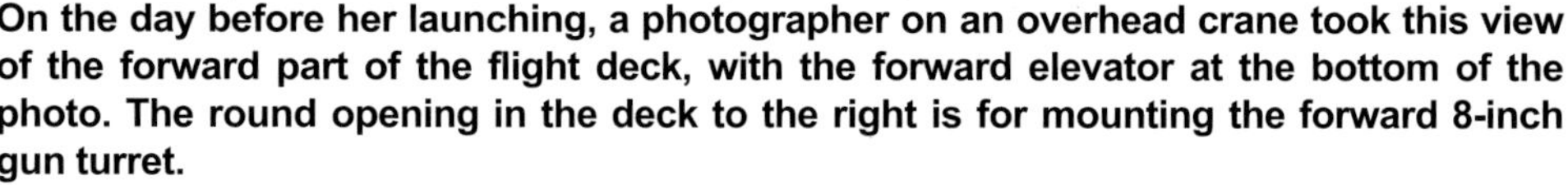

The forward elevator well, fitted with scaffolding and a temporary bulkhead, is viewed from starboard on 2 October 1925. The elevator would occupy the front part of the well, while the aft part would have two downward-folding panels at flight-deck level.

The flight deck of *Lexington* is viewed from frame 65 facing aft on 2 October 1925. The T shape of the forward elevator is apparent; the aft extension of the T was to accommodate extra-long aircraft. Temporary safety rails are on the edges of the deck.

This view of the aft elevator taken the day before launching bears the original inscription, "Elevator opening for bringing small parts from hangar deck." In time, the aft elevator would prove to be of limited use because of its small size, and both elevators were slow.

14

On 2 October 1925, with one day left to go before the launching of the *Lexington*, crews are applying shoring to immobilize the rudder and the propellers during the launching. Light-colored poppets are fitted underneath the hull, secured with fittings farther up on the sides of the hull. After launching, the poppets were removed. Written on the hull above the propellers for the benefit of the tugboat crews who will assist *Lexington* once launched is "WHEEL / KEEP CLEAR."

The stern of the *Lexington* is portrayed on the day before launching, also showing the ramp at the aft end of the flight deck. The assembly attached to the upper edge of the rudder is shoring, designed to immobilize the rudder during the stern-first launching.

The day before the launching, the *Lexington* sits poised on the ways. At the bow are three hawse pipes for three anchors. The bulbous bow was designed to optimize the flow of water around the bow and the hull, reducing drag and improving performance.

The rudder and its temporary shoring are observed from the port side on 2 October 1925. Painted in white are draft marks, indicating the distance from the keel to the waterline in feet. As built, *Lexington* had a minimum draft of 24.25 feet and a maximum of 30.5 feet.

Old Glory affixed to her bow, the *Lexington* slides down the ways on 3 October 1925. The ship was sponsored by Mrs. Theodore D. Robinson, the wife of the Assistant Secretary of the Navy. A number of people are on the flight deck for the launching.

The *Lexington* is now fully in the water upon launching, still moving rearward under the momentum of her slide into the Weymouth Fore River. With much construction left to be finished on the ship, she is riding high on the water, allowing a view of much of her armored belt. Located above and below the waterline adjacent to the vital machinery spaces within the ship, the armored belt was about nine feet and four inches high, with a width of seven inches from the top down three feet, and from there tapering to 5 inches in thickness at the bottom. (U.S. Naval Shipbuilding Museum)

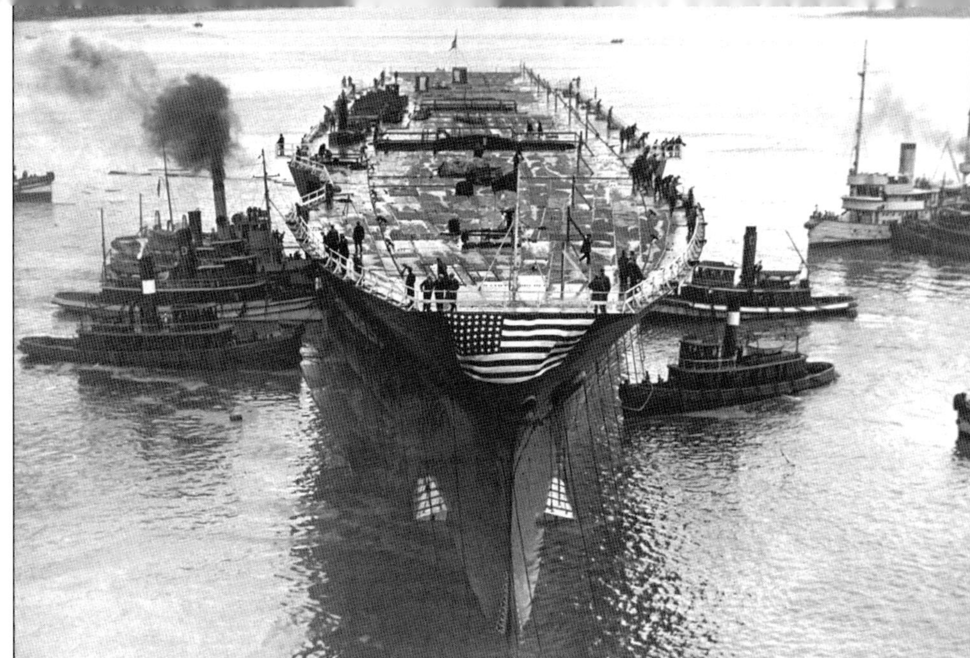

Tugboats line up alongside *Lexington* after her launching. Since the *Lexington* was unable to navigate under her own power at that point, tugboats were required to move the ship to her fitting-out dock at the Fore River Plant, where work would continue on her. (National Museum of Naval Aviation)

The flight deck of the *Lexington* is in view immediately after the launching of the ship. The openings for the forward and aft elevators are visible on the flight deck. The main-battery turrets, the superstructure or island, the smokestack, and other fixtures were yet to be installed.

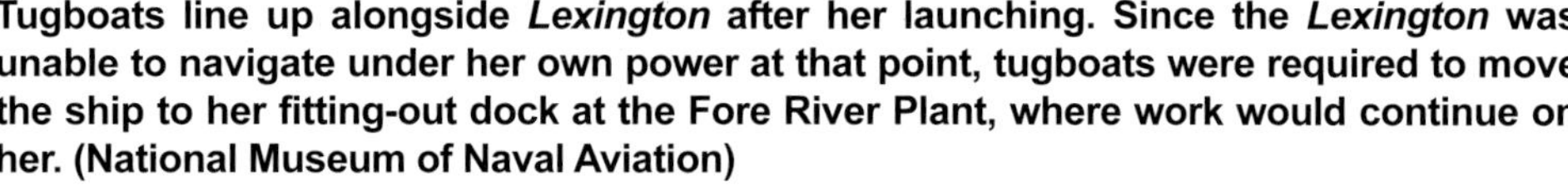

The *Lexington* moves toward her fitting-out dock at the Fore River Plant on 3 October 1925. To the right is the Argentinian battleship *Rivadavia,* built at Fore River from 1910 to 1915. At the time of *Lexington*'s launching, she was undergoing modernization there.

Civilian spectators look on and passengers line the rails on the flight deck as *Lexington* continues her short journey from building ways to fitting-out dock. Toward the top of the hull, the cutout for the yet-to-be-constructed forward starboard gun gallery is visible.

Lexington rests at her fitting-out dock at Fore River on 13 January 1926. Scaffolding is erected on a barge adjacent to the bow, and the gun gallery is under construction, with scaffolding erected below it. Scaffolding is also suspended on the bow below the front edge of the flight deck. To the right is AB-1, a crane ship that was converted from the battleship USS *Kearsarge* (BB-5). It supplemented the fixed cranes on the opposite side of the *Lexington*.

The aft port side of the *Lexington* is observed at the fitting-out dock at Fore River on 13 January 1926. Two of the four boat pockets on the port side are visible. Recessed in the hull along the main deck level just below the flight deck is the aft port gun gallery.

In a 10 April 1926 photograph of *Lexington*'s main deck facing forward, to the right are the boiler uptakes, which will later be extended up through the smokestack. In the background on the starboard side, construction of the superstructure has begun.

The flight deck of the *Lexington* is viewed from frame 120 facing aft on 15 January 1926. The frame number, mentioned often in this book, refers to the transverse frames of the ship, numbered consecutively, forward to aft. The frame number was often used to refer to a specific longitudinal point on the ship. To the left are several of the boiler uptakes, fitted with temporary covers and with guard rails surrounding them. To the right of centerline is AB-1.

The flight deck of the *Lexington* is viewed facing aft from a position adjacent to where the front of the smokestack eventually would be. To the left are the uptakes, and just aft of the one to the rear, construction of the smokestack has just started. At the center of the deck adjacent to the rear of the smokestack is the aft elevator well, covered with a tarp. Some of the wooding decking has been applied to the steel flight deck.

The smokestack is taking shape to the left in this view of the flight deck of *Lexington* looking aft on 7 July 1926. Above the flight deck, the uptakes are routed into four smoke pipes, housed inside the smokestack. Thus, there would be four outlets to the smoke pipes atop the smokestack when it was completed. At the bottom of the photo is part of the forward elevator well; a section of deck is also open aft of the well.

Lexington had four twin 8-inch/55-caliber Mk. 9 Mod. 1 gun mounts, two forward of the superstructure and two aft of the smokestack. Seen here on 7 July 1926 are the two aft mounts, trained inboard, with the smokestack under construction just forward of them.

Staging for workmen fitting out the *Lexington* surrounds the smokestack and superstructure and is hanging from the port side of the hull in a photograph taken at Fore River on 7 October 1926. The pilot house is under construction atop the superstructure.

The forward elevator well is viewed from above facing forward in another 7 July 1926 photograph. The section of deck that has not yet been installed to the rear of the well is visible. Large components were still being lowered below decks for installation, which may account for the gap in the flight deck aft of the elevator well. To the right, scaffolding encloses the superstructure, which is under construction.

A view of *Lexington* at the fitting-out dock at Fore River shows much of her port side on 4 January 1927. Forward fire-control platforms have been installed on the foremast, and the bipod-type stub mainmast with the aft fire-control towers is aft of the smokestack.

By the time this photo was taken on 7 April 1927, the bridge had been installed around the pilot house. The main-battery director top is above the pilot house, mounted on the foremast, and at the top of the foremast, the secondary-battery control top is being built.

The photographer apparently gained access to the top of the smokestack to take this view of the *Lexington* facing forward on 7 October 1926. To the right, the tripod-type foremast is under construction. Forward of the lower part of the mast is the pilot house, its top open pending the addition of the next level of the superstructure. To the left is the forward elevator well. The flap doors have been installed at the rear extension of the well; when raised, the flaps formed part of the flight deck; when lowered, they provided clearance for extra-large aircraft.

Lexington is viewed off her port bow at Fore River on 7 April 1927. At this point in time, the carrier had eight months more of fitting-out work to be completed before she would be commissioned. The compartment partway up the front of the smokestack is the secondary conning station, where the ship could be controlled if the pilot house was disabled, on top of which is the open-topped primary aviation control station, or Pri-Fly.

The smokestack and the two aft 8-inch gun turrets are viewed facing forward on 8 July 1927. Work is still underway on the aft main-battery and secondary-battery control stations on the stub mainmast aft of the smokestack. The turrets had three doors per side.

In the interim since the similar photograph of *Lexington* was taken on 7 April 1927, in this 8 July 1927 photo the top of the foremast has been installed and scaffolding has been removed from the side of the smokestack. Three months remain until commissioning.

The foremast and the upper part of the *Lexington*'s superstructure and control platforms are viewed from the rear, 8 July 1927. The level to the front, where the legs of the foremast pass down through the platform, is the navigating-bridge level. The aft legs of the foremast straddle the charthouse, which is just aft of the pilothouse. On the extension of the platform at the rear of this level, the standard, or master, compass is visible.

On 4 October 1927, fitting-out of the *Lexington* is advancing. The boom of the aircraft crane is propped up on blocks in the left foreground. Situated on top of the pilot house is the 20-foot rangefinder. A substantial amount of ship's rigging has been installed.

The forward elevator well is at bottom left of this look at the forward part of *Lexington's* flight deck on 4 October 1927. The light-colored strips running across the flight deck are the palisade: hinged slats that could be raised to shield the aircraft from wind currents.

The smokestack of *Lexington* is viewed from the front in a 4 October 1927 photograph. Midway up the front of the stack is the secondary conning station, an enclosed compartment with large windows. Directly above this station is the primary aviation control station, Pri-Fly. This station was where air operations on the carrier were controlled under the supervision of the air officer. It was open-topped for better visibility.

The exterior of the *Lexington,* seen here on 13 October 1927, had been painted between early July and early October in a scheme of # 5 Standard Navy Gray, with the flight deck stained in a mahogany or maroon color and steel decks painted Dark Gray.

Lexington, center, is viewed from the front in another 13 October 1927 aerial view. The contrast of the stained flight deck with the Navy Gray steel structures is apparent. Today, the heavy cruiser USS *Salem* (CA-139) is on permanent display in this part of the yard.

Lexington's port amidships is viewed close-up toward the end of her fitting-out period. A good view is provided of one of the boat pockets. The structure on the bottom of the 8-inch gun control compartment above the pilot house is the radio-compass booth. (San Diego Air and Space Museum)

Another view of part of *Lexington*'s port side shows all four boat pockets on that side of the ship. A key difference between *Lexington* and her sister ship *Saratoga* was that the Sara had a catwalk halfway up each side of the smokestack, while *Lexington* did not. (San Diego Air and Space Museum)

Appearing in a nearly pristine Navy Gray paint scheme, *Lexington* rests dockside at the Fore River Shipyard around the time of her December 1927 commissioning. All three anchors are now present, including one on each side of the bow and one on the centerline of the bow. Above the anchors are two hawse holes for mooring lines. The snubbed-off shape of the forward end of the flight deck is apparent. Life nets are rigged along the edges of the flight deck. (San Diego Air and Space Museum)

Lexington was photographed off her port stern in this undated photo probably taken in the late fall of 1927. The ship is nearly complete, but work still continues, and scaffolding is present, including along the hull and around the main mast aft of the smokestack.

Lexington is viewed from a lower angle toward the end of her fitting-out period. On the port side of the hull, boat booms are in their stowed positions. On the stern are three booms for rigging a life net. Several of the stern doors, used by line handlers when tying up, are open. (Boston Public Library)

At the conclusion of the fitting-out period at Fore River Shipyard, officers and crew are assembled on the flight deck of the *Lexington* for her commissioning ceremony. The ship now was entitled to bear the designation USS, United States Ship, before her name. (San Diego Air and Space Museum)

The U.S. flag is hoisted on the aft end of USS *Lexington*'s flight deck during the commissioning ceremony, 14 December 1927. When all of the ship's flags were hoisted simultaneously during the ceremony, it marked the formal commissioning of the ship.

USS *Lexington* rests at the fitting-out dock at Fore River Shipyard, Quincy, Massachusetts, at around the time of her December 1927 commissioning. In this view, the outline of the top of the ship's armored belt is visible amidships above the waterline. By now, the 5-inch/25-caliber Mk. 10 Mod. 1 gun mounts had been installed on the four galleries just below the flight deck; three gun mounts were on each gallery, with two galleries on each side of the ship. (National Museum of Naval Aviation)

A photograph taken from one of the forward fire-control tops of the *Lexington* on 20 December 1927 documents the appearance of the forward part of the flight deck six days after her 14 December commissioning. The palisade has been erected on the deck to the port side of the forward 8-inch gun turret. A round platform with safety rails for a machine gun mount is on the roof of the second 8-inch turret. Toward the front of the flight deck are catapult tracks for launching seaplanes.

The smokestack and mid-to-aft part of the flight deck of the *Lexington* are the subjects of this 20 December 1927 photograph taken from one of the forward fire-control tops. Toward the bottom is a platform with four 6-pounder saluting guns. Farther up on the front of the smokestack is the secondary conning station and Pri-Fly. A plank for a workman is suspended over the side of the secondary conning station. In the background, the aft elevator well is visible. Life nets are erected around the flight deck.

Tugboats assist USS *Lexington* as she leaves the fitting-out area at Fore River Shipyard, 5 January 1928. In the background is the Washington Street swing bridge, standing open to admit the aircraft carrier. A boat is visible in each of the three boat pockets seen here.

Moments after the preceding photo was taken, the *Lexington* has cleared the swing bridge and is ready to navigate the series of bays between Quincy and her next destination, dry dock at the South Boston Navy Yard Annex, where her lower hull will be painted. (National Museum of Naval Aviation)

The *Lexington* slips by the Washington Street swing bridge as she departs the Fore River Shipyard on 5 January 1928. From this angle, it can be seen that the secondary conning station on the front of the smokestack was not entirely enclosed but was open at the rear. (National Museum of Naval Aviation)

A tradition in the U.S. Navy is for newly commissioned ships to receive a silver service. Civic officials of Lexington, Massachusetts, presented the USS *Lexington* with her set when the carrier was in dry dock at South Boston Navy Yard Annex in early 1928. (San Diego Air and Space Museum)

The *Lexington* enters dry dock number three at South Boston Navy Yard Annex on 11 January 1928. Numbers of hawsers running from the ship are secured to the dock in order to position the ship in the proper place before the water is pumped out of the dry dock.

Lexington is viewed from an elevated position, probably on the movable crane seen in the photograph at left, as the vessel is positioned in dry dock three at South Boston Navy Yard Annex. The catapult tracks for launching seaplanes are visible on the flight deck.

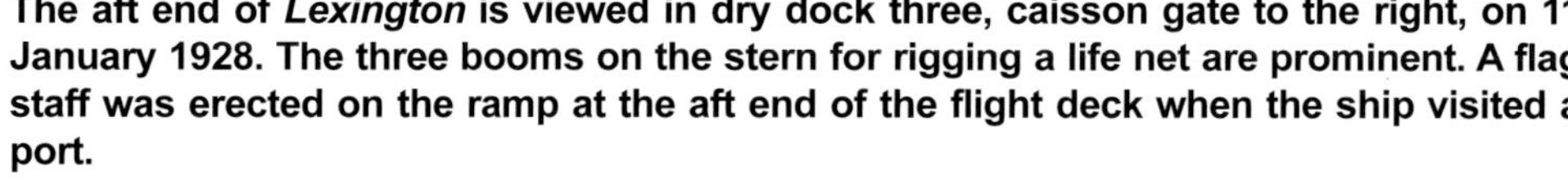

The aft end of *Lexington* is viewed in dry dock three, caisson gate to the right, on 11 January 1928. The three booms on the stern for rigging a life net are prominent. A flag staff was erected on the ramp at the aft end of the flight deck when the ship visited a port.

As water is pumped out of dry dock three on 11 January 1928, men in boats scrape marine growth that has accumulated below the waterline on the hull of *Lexington*. The object was to remove marine growth quickly, since it would harden once exposed to air. (National Museum of Naval Aviation)

Dry dock three at the South Boston Navy Yard Annex is almost free of water. A close examination of the photograph reveals that aft of the bow there are still workmen on boats at the turn of the hull. A good view is also provided of the bulbous bow. (Boston Public Library)

As *Lexington* is prepared for post-commissioning work on her lower hull at dry dock three at the South Boston Annex, several men to the lower left, apparently photographers, pack up their tripods. Dry dock three was one of the largest dry docks on the East Coast. (Boston Public Library)

All of the water has been extracted from the dry dock on 11 January 1928. Keel blocks below the ship's keel and bilge blocks at intervals to the sides of the keel supported the ship in dry dock, allowing painters and workmen to access the underside of the hull. (Boston Public Library)

Dwarfed by the enormous size if the vessel before them, workmen on the floor of the dry dock near the bow are scraping the hull and apparently assessing the scale of the work yet to be done. In the background at the bottom of the hull is the curved shape of the port bilge keel, meant to counteract the ship's tendency to roll.

The port side of the rudder and the port inboard propeller of the *Lexington* are in view in this photo taken during the ship's dry-docking in early January 1929. When a U.S. Navy ship was dry-docked, it was routine to inspect the propellers and check their pitch.

The two port propellers of the *Lexington* are shown while the ship is dry-docked on 11 January 1928. Also in view are the propeller brackets or struts and propeller shafts. Underneath the keel, the keel blocks that supported the weight of the ship are visible.

The stern of the *Lexington* is viewed in dry dock three at the South Boston Annex. Staging has been erected to give workmen access to all four propellers. On the stern above the hinge points at the bottoms of the three life-net booms are line-handler doors, shown in the closed positions. Hanging from the undersides of the aft part of the flight deck are four kedge anchors, two per side. These were used to prevent the ship from swinging around the forward anchor. (San Diego Air and Space Museum)

The first of a series of three photos of the port side of the *Lexington* around early 1928 shows features from the aircraft crane to the left to the aft 8-inch gun turret to the right. All four boat pockets on the port side are in view, but no ship's boats are present. (Boston Public Library)

Details of the designs of the port side of the island, foremast, forward and aft fire-control tops, the smokestack, and the aft 8-inch turrets are visible. The interior of the aft elevator well is painted white, contrasting with the mahogany or maroon stain on the flight deck. (Boston Public Library)

After *Lexington* completed her time in dry dock at the South Boston Annex in early 1928, she began receiving her aircraft. Parked just aft of the aft elevator on the *Lexington* is a Martin T3M torpedo bomber with markings for Torpedo Squadron 1B (VT-1B). (Boston Public Library)

In early 1928 civilians look over planes of the *Lexington*'s air group, apparently on a dock preparatory to embarking on the carrier. To the right is Curtiss F6C-3 Hawk bureau number (BuNo) A-7153, side number 5-F-16, of Fighting Squadron 5A (VF-5A). (San Diego Air and Space Museum)

During her shakedown cruise in early 1928, *Lexington* stopped in Newport, Rhode Island, to take on equipment and ordnance, including torpedoes for her torpedo bombers. Here, crewmen ease a torpedo down onto a trolley on the flight deck of the *Lexington*. (San Diego Air and Space Museum)

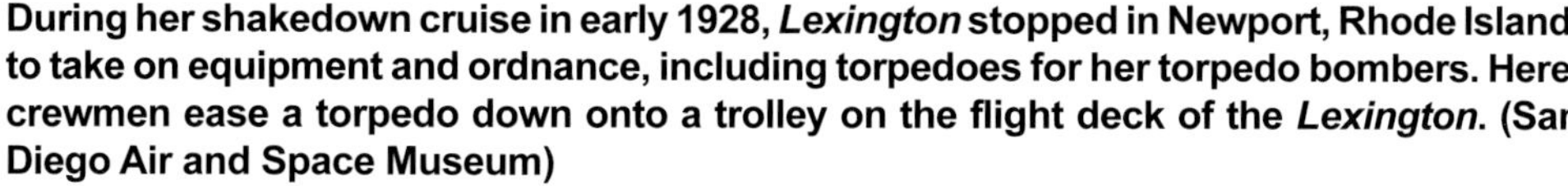

During early 1928 sailors remove snow from the flight deck of the *Lexington*. The man to the right is holding a shovel marked "V-2," indicating it was the property of the V-2 division, which was responsible for aircraft-handling operations on the hangar deck. (San Diego Air and Space Museum)

Crewmen push a torpedo from one of *Lexington*'s elevators onto a deck. The warhead is not installed. As built, the ship had two torpedo workshops and storage compartments, located on the main deck and the upper half deck just forward of the forward elevator. (San Diego Air and Space Museum)

Crewmen shovel snow from the forward part of *Lexington*'s flight deck. Stretching across the deck adjacent to the forward 8-inch turret is the raised palisade, with several of its slats left lowered to provide a passageway for deck crewmen through the palisade. (Boston Public Library)

CV-2 *Lexington* General Data

Dimensions

Length, overall, as built	888 feet 6 inches
Length between perpendiculars	850 feet
Maximum beam:	130 feet 1½ inch
Waterline beam, as built:	105 feet 5¼ inches
Waterline beam, post-1936:	111 feet 9 inches
Flight Deck dimensions, 1941:	866 feet 2 inches x 105 feet 11¼ inches
Hangar Deck:	393 feet x 68 feet x 20 feet
Draft, max, as built:	31 feet 10⅜ inches
Displacement, light:	34,067 tons
Displacement, standard:	41,187 tons
Displacement, full load, 1936:	43,054 tons
Displacement, full load, 1942:	47,879 tons

Machinery

Total weight:	6,894 tons
Boilers:	16 Yarrow; 295 psi, 522° Fahrenheit
Propulsion turbo-generators:	General Electric, squirrel cage, rotor-wound, 5,000 volt, two per shaft
Shaft Horsepower:	212,702 during trial; 180,000 design
Maximum speed:	34.99 knots trial; 33.25 knots design
Lighting/ship's service power plant:	6 General Electric 750kW turbo-generators
Emergency lighting:	3 x 60kW, 440V, 2-phase Diesel generators
Endurance:	10 knots: 10,950 miles
Fuel:	2,637 tons oil
Aviation fuel:	137,450 gallons

Armor

Main belt:	5 to 7 inches
Flight and Hangar deck:	0 inches
Protective deck:	2 inches
Conning tower:	80-lb STS
Ship's complement, as designed:	148 officers, 1,500 men
Ship's complement, 1938:	79 officers, 1,354 men
Ship's complement, 1941:	82 officers, 1509 men
Air wing, 1941:	197 officers, 664 enlisted

Armament

1927:	8 8-inch/55 caliber; 12 5-inch/25 caliber
1941:	8 8-inch/55 caliber; 12 5-inch/25 caliber; 5 3-inch/50 caliber; 8 .50 caliber BMG
1942:	12 5-inch/25 caliber, 12 1.1-inch/75 caliber quad mounts; 22 20mm; 20 .50 caliber BMG

On the flag staff at the aft end of the flight deck of the USS *Lexington* around early 1928, a chaplain's pennant flies above the United States flag. The chaplain's pennant was flown above the flag of the United States during church services for naval personnel conducted aboard a U.S. Navy ship. The chaplain's pennant was white with a dark blue Latin cross oriented sideways. It was the only flag or pennant that could be flown above the U.S. flag. (Boston Public Library)

Tugboats assist the *Lexington* to maneuver into position in Boston Harbor around early 1928. The weather is chilly, judging by the blue coats the sailors on deck are wearing. On the side of the ship at the main-deck level, above the smokestack of the second tugboat from the right, the ship's name is spelled-out. The name *Lexington* also was on the corresponding location on the opposite side of the ship.

In a scene possibly taken on the same occasion as the preceding photograph, tugboats crowd around *Lexington*, helping her move into position. It is possible that a censor airbrushed this photo to hide certain details, such as the aft elevator, since much of the flight deck is devoid of details, whereas other details are clearly visible. When the *Lexington* entered service, the Navy discouraged the taking of aerial views of her. (San Diego Air and Space Museum)

Another photo probably taken at Boston Harbor in early 1928 shows the *Lexington* being assisted by tugboats. On the edge of the gun gallery on the main-deck level above the forwardmost tugboat are three semicircular platform extensions in the stowed positions.

Two antique cannon at a harbor fortress stand guard mutely as the USS *Lexington* passes by. The date and location of the photograph are not noted, but it probably was taken in the waters around Boston during *Lexington*'s shakedown cruises in early 1928. (Boston Public Library)

Unlike *Saratoga*, which had a catwalk midway up each side of the smokestack, *Lexington* had a catwalk on the starboard side only, as seen in this photograph. Farther up on the side of the smokestack are two searchlight platforms, accessible by ladders from the catwalk.

In a companion piece to the preceding photo, three tugboats accompany the *Lexington* in a harbor on a wintry day. Forward of the boat pocket on the starboard side of the hull were 28 doors; although it is a clearly frigid day, many of those doors are open. (Boston Public Library)

Lexington's bow pointing into the wind, a biplane takes off from the flight deck. The first flight from *Lexington* occurred on 5 January 1928, during the carrier's trip from Fore River to South Boston Annex, when Mel Pride flew a Vought UO-1 off the ship. (San Diego Air and Space Museum)

As an aircraft comes in for a landing on *Lexington*, the two types of arrestor wires the ship originally was fitted with are visible: lateral wires, which the plane tried to grab with its arrestor hook, and longitudinal wires supported by "fiddle bridge" supports. (San Diego Air and Space Museum)

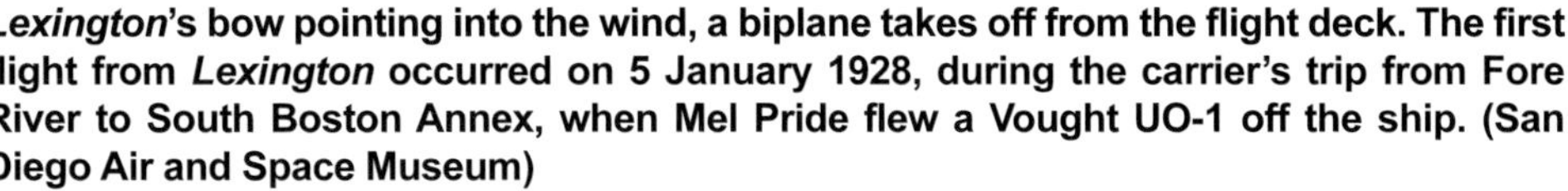

Aircraft are lined up on the flight deck of the *Lexington* around 1928 as sailors and officers dressed in whites stand by. Several of the planes have markings for VF-3B on top of their wings. The planes in the foreground exhibit aileron locks on the lower wings. (National Museum of Naval Aviation)

A view of the hangar deck in 1928 gives a sense of the dimensions of the massive hangar several decks below the main deck. Compartments on each side of the deck limited the width of the hangar. Parked on the forward part of the hangar deck are F6C-3s of VF-5B. (National Museum of Naval Aviation)

Wings folded, two Martin T3M-2 torpedo bombers of Torpedo Squadron 1B (VT-1B) are parked on the hangar deck of USS *Lexington*. The T3M-2 to the right is BuNo A-7236. In the foreground a chain railing prevents crewmen from inadvertently falling into the elevator pit. (San Diego Air and Space Museum)

In 1928, Martin T4M-1s of Torpedo Squadron 1 (VT-1B) are being spotted in place on the flight deck of the *Lexington* while another T4M-1 with wings folded is being brought up on an elevator. The T4M-1 was similar to the T3M except with a radial engine.

In January 1928, *Lexington*, originally slated to become flagship of the Scouting Fleet in the Atlantic, was ordered to join the Battle Fleet, based at Long Beach, California. The voyage included a transit of the Panama Canal, as seen here on 25 March 1928.

Sailors in *Lexington*'s forward port 5-inch/25-caliber gun gallery watch the proceedings during the transit of the Gatún Locks on 25 March 1928. The guns are at maximum elevation. The locks could barely accommodate the ship, with feet to spare on each side. (National Museum of Naval Aviation)

Lexington navigates through a cut in the Panama Canal in late March 1928. The photograph was taken from the port wing of the forward secondary, or 5-inch, control station atop the foremast, facing aft. Protruding from the smokestack is the range light. (National Museum of Naval Aviation)

Sailors dressed in whites line the rails as the *Lexington* prepares to enter the Pedro Miguel Locks of the Panama Canal. Two small boats are stowed on the flight deck, and to the right of center on the forward part of the deck, the tracks of the catapult are visible.

It is a tight squeeze as *Lexington* negotiates the Miraflores Locks of the Panama Canal on 25 March 1928. Visible to the front of the two boats on the flight deck in this photo and the preceding one is a removable mast that held at its top the masthead light.

The stern of USS *Lexington* is viewed as the carrier transits the Miraflores Locks on 25 March 1928. The three life-net booms on the stern would be removed from the ship sometime during the next year. A door is open next to the center boom.

After reporting to the Battle Fleet's headquarters at Long Beach, California, in early April 1928, the *Lexington* proceeded to Hunters Point drydocks at San Francisco for repairs and maintenance. In this photograph the carrier is seen in dry dock number three at Hunters Point on 19 April. The building with the curved side adjacent to the *Lexington* is building number 140, the pump house for dry dock number three. (National Museum of Naval Aviation)

A photo dated 21 April 1928 shows the *Lexington* in dry dock at Hunters Point from the aft port quarter. Two vertical shores or braces support the weight of the stern. Staging planks for the workmen are suspended from rigging attached to fittings built into the hull. Farther up on the side of the hull are two boat booms in their stowed positions. The brackets on the hull to which the heels, or bottoms, of those booms are hinged are visible.

Lexington, center, is viewed in dry dock number three at Hunters Point in a photograph dated 19 April 1928. A close examination of the flight deck suggests that crewmen were applying new stain to it. To the left, another ship is in dry dock number two.

Lexington is viewed from the front in dry dock three at Hunters Point. Between the dry docks, the structure with the smokestack is the pump house that extracted the water from dry dock number two. Both dry docks still exist.

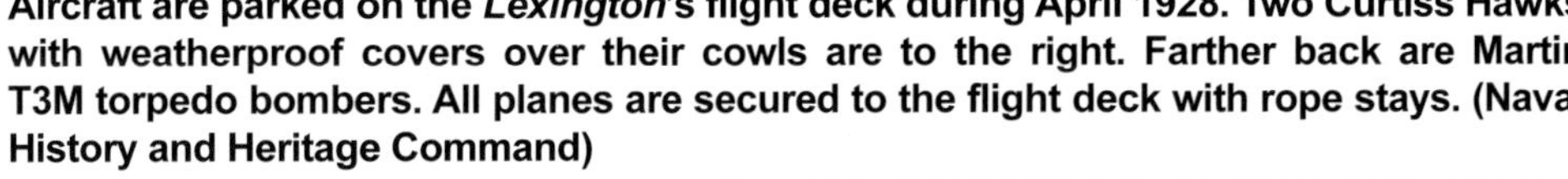

Aircraft are parked on the *Lexington*'s flight deck during April 1928. Two Curtiss Hawks with weatherproof covers over their cowls are to the right. Farther back are Martin T3M torpedo bombers. All planes are secured to the flight deck with rope stays. (Naval History and Heritage Command)

A variety of plane types are on the flight deck in this circa-1928 photo. In the foreground are Vought O2U Corsairs of VS-3B. Aft of them are three Loening Amphibians of Utility Squadron 1 (VJ-1) with landing gear that retracted into the central float structure. (San Diego Air and Space Museum)

Lexington makes a full-power run off the Southern California coast on 24 May 1928. Such test runs were conducted when the ship was new and at later intervals to check the ability of the engines and boilers to maintain full speed for over a period of time.

An aerial view of *Lexington* during a full-power run in late May 1928 shows the significant wake the ship churned up. The light-colored cross on the forward part of the flight deck was a temporary feature, possibly intended as a calibration marking.

With the palisade erected in the foreground to cut down on wind, crewmen of the *Lexington* scrub their hammocks in the time-honored naval fashion in 1928 using long-handled brushes and soapy water. They will then hang them to dry on the rails. (National Museum of Naval Aviation)

A bow-on shot of *Lexington* portrays her power as she cuts through the waves during speed trials off Southern California on 18 June 1928. The ship set a new record speed of 30 knots during the trials, but her sister ship, *Saratoga*, broke the record the next month. (National Museum of Naval Aviation)

Ship Signal Flags

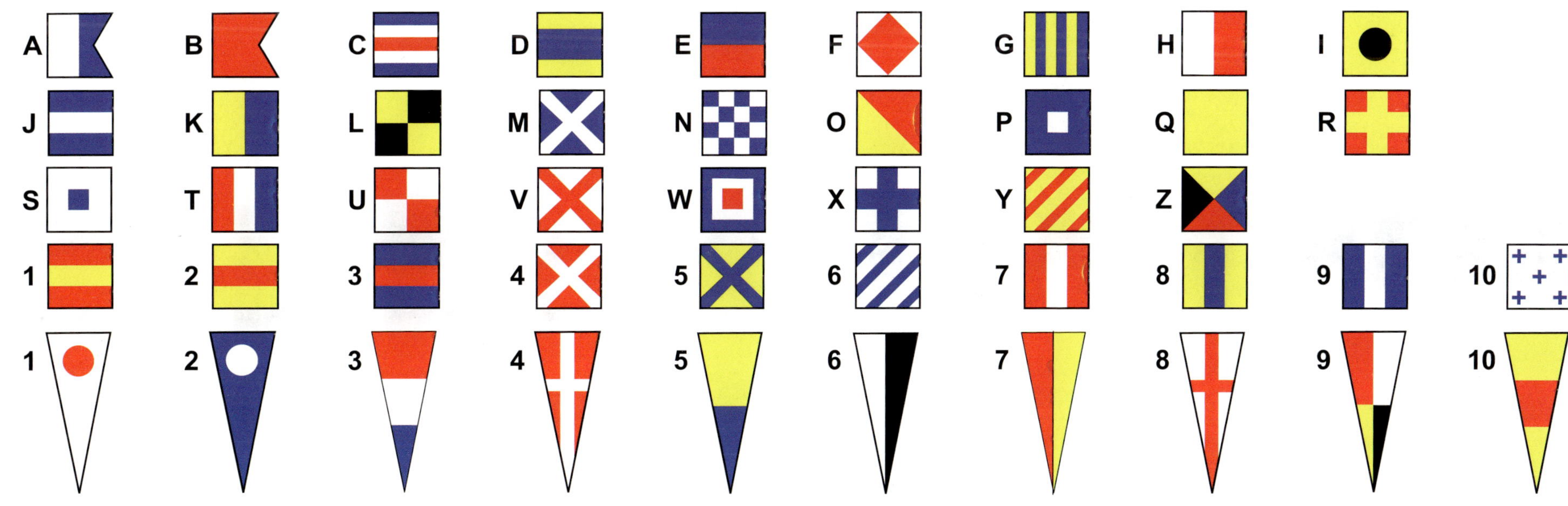

A photographer in a passing Navy plane took this shot of the port amidships area of *Lexington* in June 1928. Both of the elevators are lowered, but the flap doors immediately aft of the forward elevator are raised flush with the flight deck. When lowered, those flaps swung down at right angles into the open space in the main-deck level below. To the left, gun crewmen are gathered around the forward port 5-inch/25-caliber mounts; the aft mount is trained inboard.

Some of *Lexington*'s defensive artillery is viewed. In the foreground are the three starboard forward 5-inch/25-caliber mounts. The semicircular platform extensions were hinged so they could be stored folded up. To the rear are the forward 8-inch gun mounts. (San Diego Air and Space Museum)

Six months after her first dry-docking at Hunters Point, *Lexington* returned on 31 October 1928 for more work. The semicircular platform extensions seen lowered in the preceding photo of the starboard forward gallery are seen raised on the port forward gallery.

Toward the top of *Lexington*'s foremast is the forward secondary-battery control top, from which the 5-inch gun batteries were remotely controlled. At the bottom of the photo is the forward primary-battery control top, from which the 8-inch guns were directed.

It is Washington's Birthday, 22 February 1929, and the USS *Lexington* is in full dress, decked-out in flags and pennants fore to aft, off Panama. Dressing a ship is the Navy's way of honoring holidays and special events. Boat booms are extended from the hull.

On 7 March 1929 crewmen swab *Lexington*'s deck. One man sprays water on the wooden deck while others scrub it with long-handled brushes. With well over 100,000 square feet of area on the flight deck, swabbing this deck was a serious, time-consuming business. (National Archives via Rob Stern)

A Vought O2U-2 Corsair takes off from *Lexington* in March 1929. Although the carrier originally had a catapult for launching seaplanes, for other planes the procedure was to steer the ship into the wind, thus increasing the airflow and enabling short takeoffs.

The twin 8-inch guns of turret number one are viewed from below, with one of the guns of turret number two visible between them. The 8-inch/55-caliber designation of these guns meant that the guns had a bore of 8 inches and a length of 55 times their bore, or 440 inches. Fitted in the muzzles of the guns are tompions, large plugs that kept out salt, moisture, and foreign objects. Visible in the background, top to bottom, are the radio-compass booth, forward main-battery control top, and forward secondary-battery control top.

USS *Lexington*'s number-three twin 8-inch gun mount, immediately aft of the smokestack, is being fired during exercises. The twin 8-inch/55-caliber Mk. 9 Mod. 1 guns were normally remotely controlled by the fore and aft fire-control directors.

A photo dated 7 October 1929 shows the effects of the 8-inch guns of turret number two on a target screen. The crews of the 8-inch guns of the main battery as well as of the ship's other guns built and maintained proficiency by frequent target practice.

In October 1929 the *Lexington* made the first of many visits to the Navy Yard, Puget Sound, (NYPS) at Bremerton, Washington, for refitting, maintenance, and repairs. The carrier is shown moored to a dock at NYPS in this photo dated 14 October.

Martin T4M-1 BuNo A-7638 was assigned to the leader of the third section of VT-1B in 1929. The T4M-1 had a maximum speed of 114 m.p.h, range of 363 miles, and armament of a torpedo and one flex-mounted .30-caliber machine gun in the rear cockpit.

Curtiss F6C-3 Hawk BuNo A-7149 of VB-1B "Red Rippers" served on the *Lexington*. The F6C-4 had a maximum speed of 153 miles per hour, a range of 341 miles, and armament of two .30-caliber machine guns or one .30-caliber and one .50-caliber.

Lexington wears full dress on 27 October 1929 to celebrate Navy Day at NYPS, Bremerton. Coincidentally, the stock market crash that precipitated the Great Depression occurred just three days earlier, but NYPS would actually grow during the depression.

Several Boeing fighter planes are undergoing major overhauls on the aft end of the hangar deck around 1929. Two fuselages rest on wooden stands as mechanics work on them. In the background are several wings, including one upright at the center. (National Museum of Naval Aviation)

Boeing F3B-1 BuNo A-7720 served with VF-3B around 1929. The F3B-1 had a maximum speed of 157 miles per hour and a range of 340 miles. It was armed with two fixed .30-caliber machine guns and could carry up to 125 pounds of bombs.

In a view of part of the flight deck of the *Lexington* taken around 1929, in the foreground is a mix of Boeing F3B-1 fighter planes of VF-3B and Curtiss F6C-3 fighters of VB-1B. The F3B-1s are the planes with the radial engines with covers over them, while the F6C-3s are the ones with liquid-cooled inline engines and propeller spinners. In the background are Martin T4M-1 torpedo bombers assigned to VT-1B. The F3B-1 in the foreground with the white fuselage band was the plane of the leader of the second section of VF-3B. (National Museum of Naval Aviation)

56

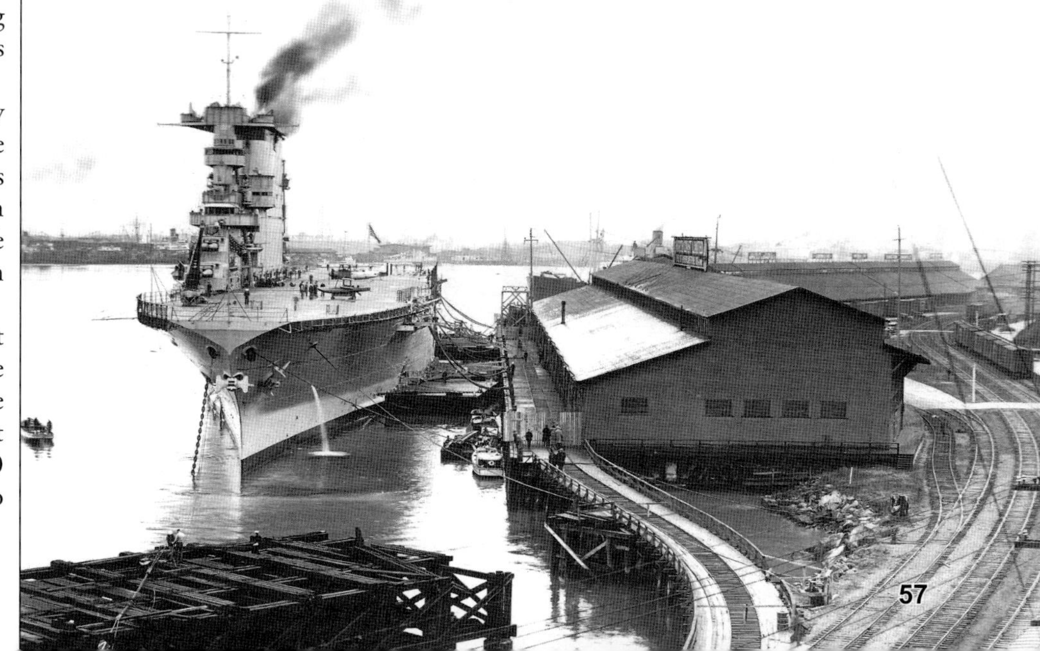

Lexington rides at anchor in Commencement Bay, Tacoma, Washington, on 16 December 1929. She was there to generate electrical power for the city, which was suffering a shortage of hydroelectric power because an extended drought had lowered her reservoirs.

In late 1929 the Pacific Northwest was suffering from a drought, one of the impacts of which was that Tacoma, Washington, a city that relied upon hydroelectric power, was drawing dangerously near blackout conditions as the waters of the Nisqually and Skokomish Rivers dropped. So serious was the problem that one of the city's biggest power users – and employers – had the power turned off by officials in order to save energy, resulting in 300 people being laid off. Nearby Fort Lewis also implemented conservation measures, darkening the barracks at 1600 hours.

The turbo-electric drive of *Lexington* and *Saratoga* was well known, having been widely touted in the press releases concerning the powerful new aircraft. Also well known was the fact that the vessels were at Puget Sound Navy Yard, roughly 40 miles away. An appeal was made to President Herbert Hoover that one of the vessels be dispatched to supply the city with power. Ultimately, a deal was concluded for *Lexington* to supply the city power at a rate of one cent per kilowatt-hour. In five days, the city of Tacoma constructed two miles of high-tension power lines, stretching from a dock to power substation.

Lexington tied up at Baker Dock in Tacoma on 15 December 1929, and two days later current that normally would run to her No. 4 aft main motor began to flow from her powerplant to the beleaguered city. In order to supply the commercial 60-cycle current, *Lexington's* main turbine had to run at 1800 r.p.m, 45 r.p.m. above the rated maximum, which it did with no apparent ill effects. She remained there, supplying power, until 17 January 1930, supplying 4,250,960 kilowatt-hours of energy in total. Subsequently, the city of Seattle, which had objected to *Lexington* servicing Tacoma, made a similar request for assistance, which was declined.

Once *Lexington* was moored at Baker Dock, Tacoma, connections were made from the carrier's bus bars to high-tension electrical lines the city had extended to that dock. *Lexington* supplied electricity to the city from 17 December 1929 to 16 January 1930. (National Museum of Naval Aviation)

An aerial view shows *Lexington* at Baker Dock on 3 January 1930, midway through her stay in Tacoma. By now, the abbreviation "LEX" had been painted on the aft end of her flight deck as an identification aid to returning pilots. A large circle was also present.

A barge holding a support made of timbers with insulators on top was placed between the port side of the *Lexington* and Baker Dock to support the electrical cables routed through the door in the side of the hull (right) to transformers temporarily located on the dock. (National Archives Seattle via Tracy White)

The support and electrical cables seen in the preceding photo are visible on the barge toward the right of this photo dated 18 December 1929, taken from the flight deck of the *Lexington*. To the center are transformer banks and circuit breakers on Baker Dock. (National Archives Seattle via Tracy White)

Lexington is moored to Baker Dock, Tacoma, on Christmas Eve 1929. During the month-long visit of the carrier to Tacoma, the ship provided the city with 4.25 million kilowatt-hours of electrical power. Complex measures were needed during the operation to ensure safety. (National Archives Seattle via Tracy White)

Lexington continues to provide electrical power to the city of Tacoma on 13 January 1930, a few days before her departure. By now, winter rains had replenished the city's reservoirs, and the dams would begin to generate hydroelectric power once again.

In a 21 February 1930 view of *Lexington,* front and center is Vought O2U 3-B-1, assigned to the squadron leader of VS-3B. At the lower left are two 6-pounder saluting guns; at the top left is the secondary conning station. (National Museum of Naval Aviation)

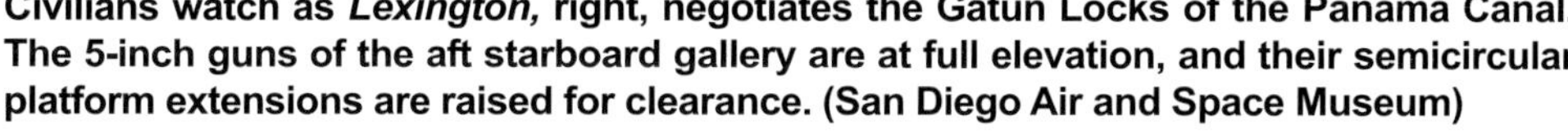

Civilians watch as *Lexington,* right, negotiates the Gatún Locks of the Panama Canal. The 5-inch guns of the aft starboard gallery are at full elevation, and their semicircular platform extensions are raised for clearance. (San Diego Air and Space Museum)

USS *Lexington* passes through the Pedro Miguel Locks of the Panama Canal on 28 February 1930 *en route* from the West Coast to the Caribbean, where she would participate with the Black Force in Fleet Problem X, war games that began on 10 March.

A rangefinder crew is at its station on one of the wings of a secondary-battery, or 5-inch gun, control top on the *Lexington* in March 1930. A rangefinder was mounted on each wing of the platform, and in the middle of the platform were two 5-inch directors.

USS *Lexington* rests at anchor at Hampton Roads, Virginia, in May 1930. A good view is provided of the configuration of the life nets that extended around the sides of the hull just below the flight deck. Crewmen are swabbing the forward part of the flight deck.

USS *Lexington* is tied up alongside Pier 15, Balboa, Canal Zone, on 29 June 1930 on her voyage west to rejoin the Pacific Fleet. The pre-WWII exercises and Fleet Problems necessitated many transits of the Panama Canal.

With aircraft wings and a radial aircraft engine framing the scene in the foreground, the upper part of the superstructure and foremast are in view. At the bottom is the aft part of the flag plot; above it are a searchlight platform and the forward gun-control tops. On the wings of the 5-inch gun-control top, enclosed with canvas windbreaks, are the two forward 5-inch rangefinders, such as the one illustrated on the preceding page.

The *Lexington* negotiates the Gatún Locks of the Panama Canal on 24 March 1931, once again bound for fleet exercises in the Caribbean. Suspended from the boom next to the smokestack is a booth for the ship's pilot, the better to con the ship thorough the locks.

During a break from maneuvers in the Caribbean on 31 March 1931, USS *Lexington* rests at anchor at the U.S. Navy base at Guantánamo Bay, Cuba. Within the next few days, the *Lexington* would commence the return trip via the Panama Canal to California.

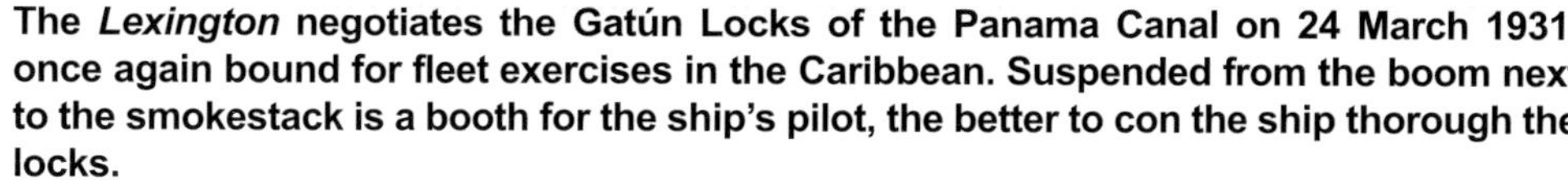

USS *Lexington* approaches a dock at Balboa, the Panama Canal Zone, on 7 April 1931 during her return trip from the Caribbean to California. Visible ahead of the bow of the *Lexington* in the distance is the forward part of USS *Saratoga*, moored at Pier 16.

Lexington and other ships of the Battle Fleet are anchored at Lahaina Roads off the west coast of Maui in mid-February 1932. The Battle Fleet recently had sailed from California to the Hawaiian Islands to participate in a fleet exercise, a simulated attack on the islands. (National Museum of Naval Aviation)

Sailors and officers of USS *Lexington* assemble for review on the after part of the flight deck in March 1932. In the left foreground are F3B-1s of VF-2B, while in the background are Martin T4M-1s of VT-1B. To the right is a plane of VF-5B. (Naval History and Heritage Command)

A March 1932 photo of the forward part of *Lexington*'s flight deck shows four Boeing F3B-1s of VF-2B in the foreground. In the background are Vought SU-2 Corsairs assigned to Marine Scouting Squadron 15 and aircraft with markings for VS-3B. (National Museum of Naval Aviation)

In a view overlooking the *Lexington*'s aft 8-inch guns, Martin T4M-1s of VT-1B warm their engines preparatory to takeoff. The date was 14 March 1932 during Fleet Problem XIII. The large circle painted on the flight deck during this period is visible.

On 11 May 1932, 15 welding machines were operated in parallel to heat the stator winding of "D" generator. The stator was the stationary part of the turbo-generator's rotor system. This arrangement of welding rigs supplied 4,000 amps at 12 volts.

Lexington is in dry dock in December 1932, and workmen are preparing the lower part of the hull for painting. The staging the men are standing on are supported by rigging attached to permanent fittings in the hull; one such fitting is above the man to the far left. (National Archives via Rob Stern)

Workmen at the Navy Yard, Puget Sound, in Bremerton, Washington, are pulling the starboard outboard propeller during a refitting and repair session in dry dock in December 1932. The cone of the propeller has been removed and is lying below the scaffolding. A chain fall is rigged above the propeller to hoist it free of its mounting. Whenever the ship was in dry dock, the propellers were carefully inspected for damage or wear.

In early 1933 the *Lexington* was in the Territory of Hawaii for Fleet Problem XIV. She is seen here off Honolulu, with Diamond Head in the distance. To the left in the second row of planes is what appears to be the Grumman XFF-1 prototype, then assigned to VF-5B.

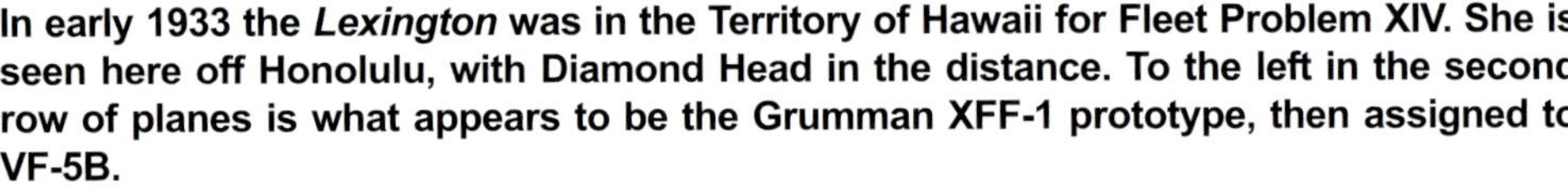

A Vought SU-2 Corsair scout plane assigned to Marine Scouting Squadron 15 (VS-15M) takes off from the *Lexington* in March 1933. At that time, VS-15M was deployed with the *Lexington*. The USMC insignia is on the side of the fuselage below the aft cockpit.

In March 1933 the *Lexington* is anchored off Long Beach, California, her air group neatly parked on the deck. Some time before this photo was taken, sister ship *Saratoga* got a vertical black stripe on each side of the smokestack to distinguish her from *Lexington*.

Martin BM-1 torpedo bomber BuNo A-8881 served with VT-1S on the *Lexington* in 1932. The BM-1 had a top speed of 146 miles per hour, range of 413 miles, and carried one fixed and one flex-mounted .30-caliber machine gun and a torpedo or a 1,000-pound bomb.

One of *Lexington*'s photographers took this moody view of the carrier docked at Bremerton, Washington, on 20 October 1933. In the 1930s *Lexington* and her sister ship *Saratoga* frequently would come to Bremerton late in the year for refitting and repairs.

In a December 1933 photo of the port side of *Lexington*'s superstructure, on the navigating bridge above the ladder next to the conning tower at lower left are red, yellow, and green lights the flight-deck control officer used to signal planes preparing to take off.

In spring 1934, *Lexington* was deployed to the East Coast. During that voyage, the ship is seen navigating the Gatún Locks of the Panama Canal on 23 April. The black paint of the band around the top of the smokestack also carried over to the top of the stack.

USS *Lexington* 1934 Plans

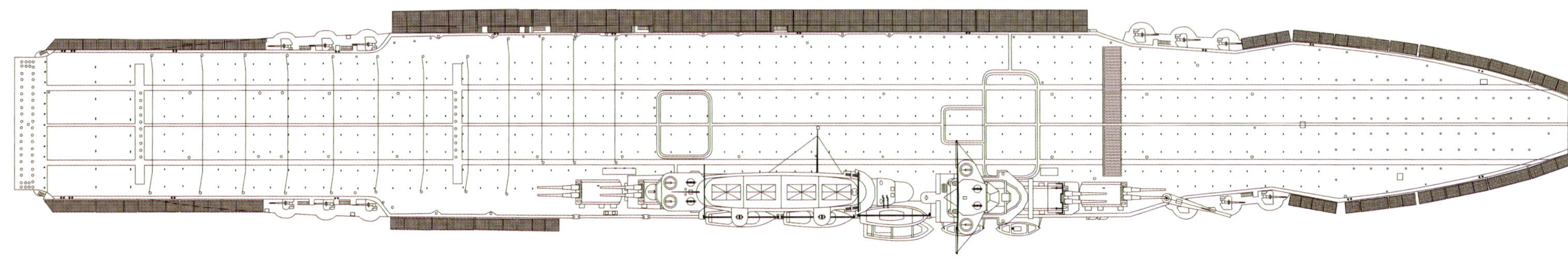

To the casual observer, the *Lexington* of 1934 was little changed from her appearance during her commissioning seven years earlier. The forward flight deck still followed the lines of her finely tapered battlecruiser bow, and – strangely for a floating airfield – few antiaircraft weapons were present. Perhaps the most visible variance from her 1927 commissioning configuration was the broad black band painted around the top of the ship's funnel, which housed the four huge uptakes that exhausted her 16 Yarrow boilers. *Lexington's* sister ship, *Saratoga,* received a broad vertical band on her funnel at the same time. These distinguishing markings were added to aid aviators in finding their "home" – with the two nearly-identical ships often operating together, aviator confusion about the vessels' identity had been an ongoing problem.

However, while little had changed externally on the ship itself, *Lexington's* main armament – her aircraft – had changed considerably during her seven years of service. For example the F3B-1, T4M-1, F6C-2/3, and O2U-2 that she had borne during the 1929 Fleet Problem IX had given way to a succession of newer aircraft such that by the time Fleet Problem XV was held in 1934, an all-new air group was being carried. For this fleet problem Lexington's VT-1B was piloting the Martin BM-1/2, VS-3B and VS-14M were both flying the Vought SU-2/3 aircraft, VF-5B was equipped with Grumman FF-1 fighters, and VF-2B was taking to the air in Boeing F4B-2 fighters.

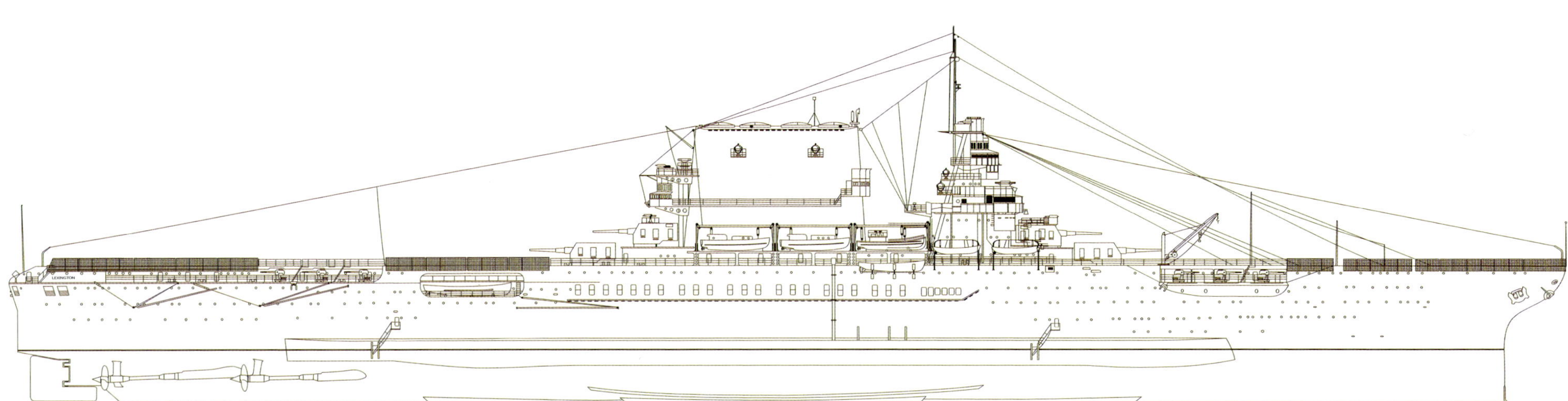

The *Lexington*'s turbo-electric propulsion gave the carrier the ability to move in reverse at speed, which also gave her the ability to launch aircraft from the rear of the flight deck, as demonstrated by a Martin BM torpedo bomber of VT-1B on 17 May 1934.

A mass of airplanes parked on the flight deck of USS *Lexington* on 26 May 1934 includes in the foreground new Grumman FF-1 fighters of VF-5B. To the lower left is the aircraft of the leader of section two of that squadron, signified by the white fuselage band.

Officers and crewmen of the *Lexington* man the rail, a naval tradition to render honors, as the ship passes in review for President Franklin Roosevelt off New York Harbor on 31 May 1934. *Lexington* was part of the largest USN peacetime armada to date.

The *Lexington* approaches the Portsmouth Navy Yard, on 13 July 1934 during her deployment that summer to the East Coast. Worthy of notice is that although the forward elevator is raised, the flap doors just aft of it are lowered.

Sister ships USS *Lexington*, left, and USS *Saratoga,* are moored at Pier 90 in Manhattan in early June 1934, hosting throngs of visitors who came down to tour the ships. Planes of their air groups were aboard, increasing the interest of a tour of the Navy's big carriers. (National Museum of Naval Aviation)

A Grumman SF-1 scout plane appears in the colors and markings of the famed VF-5B "Red Rippers" in 1934. The SF-1 had a maximum speed of 206 miles per hour, a range of 732 miles, and armament that consisted of one fixed and one flex-mounted .30-caliber machine gun.

Two months after serving as the city of Tacoma's emergency power plant, *Lexington* headed to warmer climate, steaming for the Caribbean and Fleet Problem X. *Lexington* was assigned to Black Force, which was to be the striking force, while sister *Saratoga,* as well as *Langley,* were part of the defending Blue Force. It would be five days into the problem before contact was made by the two forces, when *Lexington's* aircraft found *Saratoga* and her task force. In the mock battle that followed, *Saratoga* and *Langley* were both judged to have been rendered unable to sustain air operations. *Lexington's* aircraft, on successive strikes, were also judged to have done varying degrees of damage to other units in the Blue Force, including three battleships and a destroyer. One month later, during Fleet Problem XI, the roles of aggressor and defender were reversed, with *Lexington* defending in a mock war involving many islands in the Caribbean. This exercise indicated a need for additional scouting aircraft, with longer ranges and shorter take-off rolls.

On 16 February 1931 the Navy began conducting another of these exercises, Fleet Problem XII. *Lexington* along with sister ship *Saratoga* formed part of the defending Blue Fleet, poised against the bulk of the Navy's battleships augmented by the carrier *Langley,* as the Black force. The Black Fleet was intent on capturing the Panama Canal and a theoretical canal in Nicaragua. Once the exercise ended in March, all three carriers passed through the Panama Canal bound for more exercises off Cuba. On the last day of the month, *Lexington,* under the command of Captain King, was directed to assist Navy and Marine units with relief operations following a devastating earthquake that had struck Managua on 31 March and was followed by a major fire. This was the first time a U.S. carrier rendered aid following an overseas natural disaster.

The Army-Navy Joint Grand Exercise 4 held in February of 1932, should have served as a wake-up call for things to come. *Lexington* and *Saratoga,* under command of Rear Admiral Harry Yarnell, struck Hawaii on a series of mock attacks that began on Sunday morning, 7 February, with results judged "very impressive" by the exercise umpires.

On 3 November 1933, the White House announced that the entire U.S. fleet would visit the East Coast in 1934. In time, the sailing date of 9 April 1934 was slated, and on that day the 104 ships and 46,000 men under command of Admiral David Sellers set off for the East Coast. *En route* to Panama, the force was divided into two mock fleets, and war games were conducted along the way, ending with a simulated attack on the Army defenders of Panama. The games concluded, it took 47 hours for the armada to pass through the Panama Canal. Once in the Caribbean, further fleet exercises ensued, until finally on 25 May 1934 the fleet, including *Lexington,* swung toward New York City, where it arrived, enveloped in fog, in the dark morning hours of 31 May.

With the fog lifted, and the sun in the sky, the fleet formed a column and passed before President Franklin Roosevelt, who reviewed the fleet from the cruiser *Indianapolis* (CA-35). Admiral Sellers' flagship, the battleship *Pennsylvania* (BB-38), led the fleet, followed by *Saratoga,* with her two destroyer plane guards, and then the *Lexington,* and her plane guards. After passing the *Indianapolis, Saratoga* and *Lexington* turned into the wind and launched a combined 185 aircraft. Once the air operations were complete, both carriers tied up to Pier 90 in New York City, where they would remain, open to the public for tours, until 19 June.

Aircraft crowd the hangar deck of USS *Lexington* around 1935. To the left are several aircraft fuselages suspended from the ceiling of the hangar. The practice of stowing aircraft overhead in the hangar as a space-saving measure was called tricing. (San Diego Air and Space Museum)

Lexington is observed from her port side on 5 June 1935 toward the end of Fleet Problem XVI, which saw the carrier operating in Hawaiian waters with the fleet. Within a few months, *Lexington* would undergo a refit that would give her smokestack a different look.

Arrestor hook extended, a Grumman SF-1 scout plane piloted by a Commander Webb comes in for a landing on USS *Lexington* on 12 May 1935. Although the side number of the aircraft is difficult to discern, it is likely this plane was assigned to VS-3B.

A Grumman F2F-1 fighter takes off from *Lexington* on 31 May 1935. This aircraft probably was assigned to VF-2B, which is known to have been flying the F2F-1 from the *Lexington* at that time. In the background is a Grumman JF-1 Duck amphibian plane.

In the late summer of 1935 the *Lexington* underwent a refitting at the Navy Yard, Puget Sound, Bremerton, Washington, the main focus of which was the ship's antiaircraft defenses, with five machine gun platforms being added to the ship. Four platforms were built onto the sides of the hull below the level of the flight deck, two near the stern and two near the bow. Each of these was intended to hold four .50-caliber machine gun mounts. A fifth platform encircled the upper part of the smokestack and was designed to hold six .50-caliber machine guns per side. The smokestack platform and the forward starboard platform are visible in this photo taken on 25 September 1935 at Bremerton. (National Archives via Rob Stern)

During the summer of 1935 *Lexington* entered Puget Sound Navy Yard for a major refitting, focused chiefly on her antiaircraft defenses. Ironically, given their nature, U.S. carriers up to this point had had minimal antiaircraft defenses. When *Lexington* entered the Navy Yard at Puget Sound in 1935, her antiaircraft machine gun battery was a meager .50 caliber machine gun atop each of the superfiring 8-inch turrets. During the 1935 yard period *Lexington's* armament was augmented by a machine gun platform encircling the funnel at the fifth level, with six .50-caliber machine guns mounted on the port side of the funnel, and a like number on the starboard. At the same time, the machine guns atop the 8-inch turrets were removed. Beyond the funnel mounting, an even more noticeable change was the installation of machine gun platforms on either side of the flight deck near the ends. Each of these platforms could accommodate up to four of the machine guns.

The next year *Lexington* reentered Puget Sound for further, even more noticeable, alterations. The forward portion of the flight deck was substantially widened. The rationale was that by virtue of the ship's turbo electric drive and hull design, she could make essentially the same speed both ahead and astern. Aircraft are normally launched over the bow and recovered over the stern, the airflow over the ship aiding the aircraft's lift. Widening the flight deck forward and installing additional arrestor gear would allow *Lexington* to recover aircraft over the bow while backing at full speed, in the event of emergency.

Further modernization was planned for *Lexington* and her sister ship *Saratoga,* and in June 1939, Congress appropriated $15 million for the work, but with the outbreak of war in Europe the Navy was unwilling to sideline its two largest carriers for 11 months. Thus, work on *Lexington* was now postponed.

In a bow-on view on 25 September 1935, the new forward machine gun platforms jut from the sides of the hull with temporary staging rigged below them. The radio-compass booth has been removed from below the 8-inch gun control compartment. (National Archives via Rob Stern)

The new aft port machine gun platform on the *Lexington*, just forward of the ship's name plate, is viewed facing forward. Below the platform is temporary staging. The new machine gun platform around the upper part of the funnel is visible in the distance. (National Archives via Rob Stern)

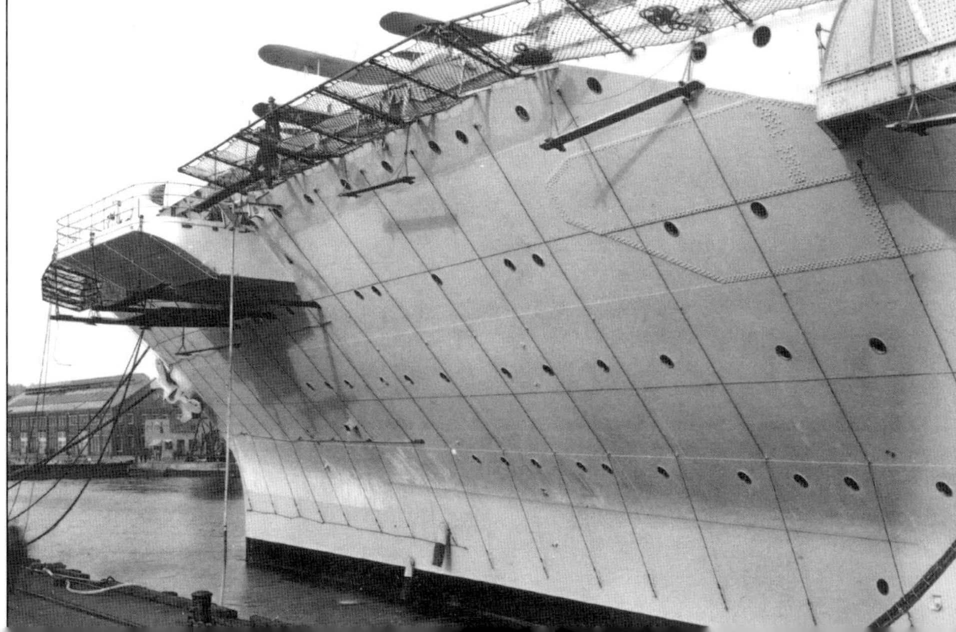

Another photo taken on 24 September 1935 to document the new construction on the *Lexington* shows the forward port machine gun platform. The 28 .50-caliber machine gun mounts added during this refitting would provide a close-range defense against aircraft. (National Archives via Rob Stern)

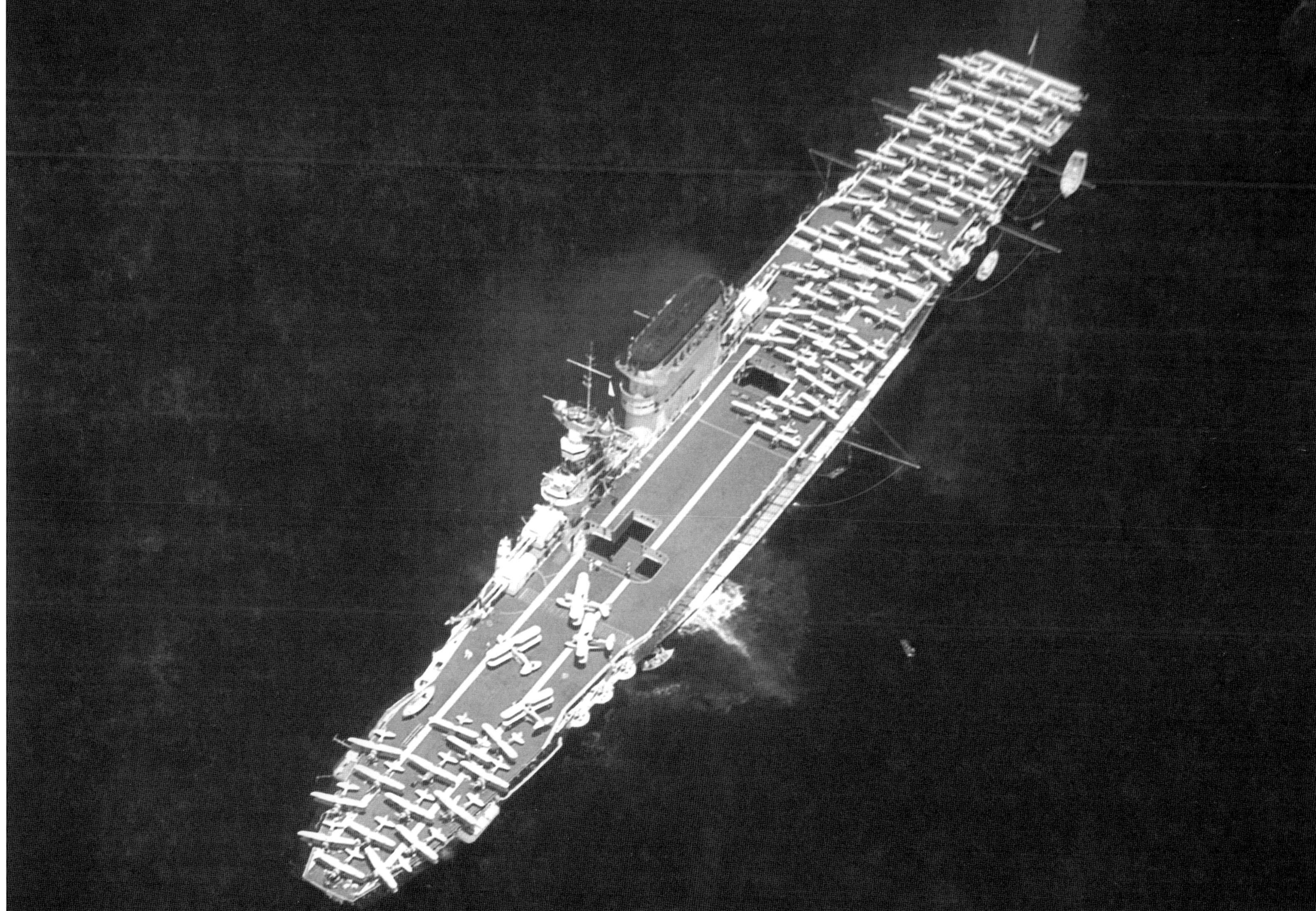

The *Lexington* lies at anchor off the coast of Panama on 11 May 1936 during Fleet Problem XVII. During these annual fleet exercises, the crew of the *Lexington* would gain crucial experience that would serve them and the rest of the Navy well when war came. The *Lexington* was still carrying several seaplanes, and two of them are parked to the front of the forward elevator. Both that elevator and the flap doors aft of it are lowered, exposing the T shape of the elevator well.

Stretching in multiple columns practically from one end of the 866-foot flight deck to the other, most of *Lexington's* 2,000-man crew stand at attention, as they receive an Admiral's inspection at Coronado Roads, California, in October 1936. The ship's aircraft have been positioned along the edges of the flight deck.

Off Long Beach, California, on 17 September 1936, a Goodyear blimp hovers over USS *Lexington* as the ship's crew, dressed in whites, spells out "NAVY" on the flight deck. The machine gun platform on the smokestack casts a shadow on the side of the stack. (National Museum of Naval Aviation)

On 12 November 1936 the *Lexington* steams through San Francisco Bay, passing Alcatraz Island and the then three-year-old prison in the background. The ship paid a visit to the area to participate in the opening of the San Francisco-Oakland Bay Bridge, which was opened to traffic on that date.

USS *Lexington* 1937 Refit

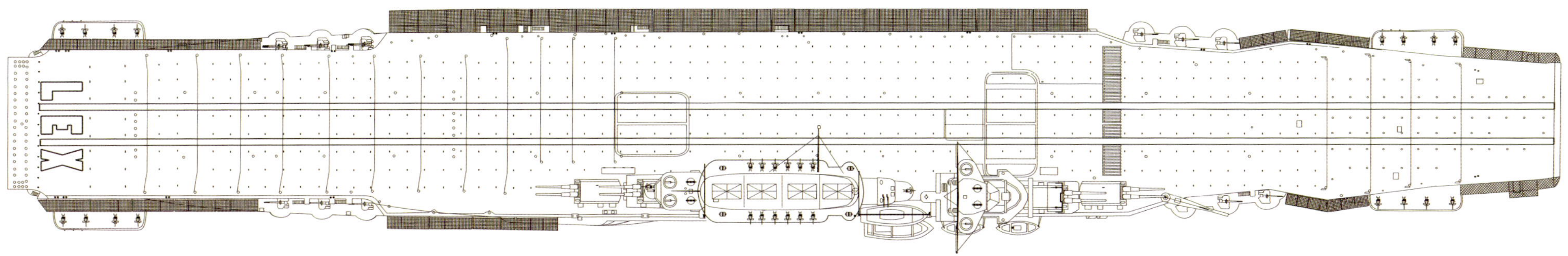

The most significant change in *Lexington's* appearance prior to World War II, and some would argue the most significant change altogether, was the result of a late 1936-early 1937 refit at Puget Sound. One of the most significant modifications made during that refit involved the widening of the flight deck forward and the installation of additional arrestor gear. These changes allowed flight operations to be conducted from either end of the ship. Previously, the narrow forward flight deck was fine for launching aircraft, but recovering aircraft over the bow was challenging, even more so with the lack of arresting wires oriented for this purpose.

Throughout her career *Lexington* most often steamed from California ports. For overhaul and heavy maintenance, she typically ventured north to Washington's Navy Yard Puget Sound. In 1936, *Lexington* tied up to the dock at the massive complex where she underwent significant modifications and flight deck changes. (National Archives Seattle via Tracy White)

During a refitting at the Navy Yard, Puget Sound, in early 1937, the front end of *Lexington's* flight deck was widened. This modification made landings feasible on the front of the flight deck, and arrestor gear was installed there as well. On the forward end of the flight deck, several Grumman airplanes are visible, probably F2F-1s. Aft of the gun gallery, above the waterline, is a door in the hull with an access ladder where boats could embark and disembark passengers. (U.S. Naval Shipbuilding Museum)

78

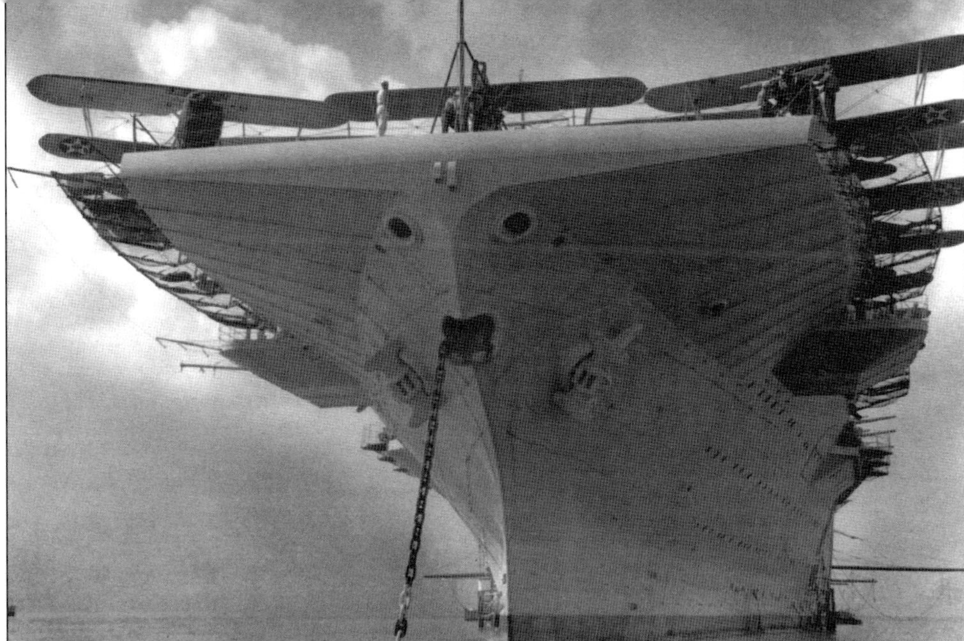

In this photo of the *Lexington* from off her bow, the center anchor has been lowered. The three forward anchors were raised and lowered by a windlass located on the main deck just below the forward part of the flight deck. Chain lockers were below the windlass. (National Museum of Naval Aviation)

A March 1937 photo shows a landing signal officer's platform and windscreen along the forward part of the flight deck. This station was designed for use in case damage to the aft part of the flight deck necessitated recovery of aircraft on the front of the deck.

Crash barriers were the last resort for stopping a landing aircraft should the aircraft fail to catch an arrestor wire with its hook. To the left of center in this photo is the port number-three crash barrier stanchion, from which the barrier wires were rigged. Behind the stanchion is some of the combination life net/windbreaker mounted alongside parts of the flight deck. The crisscrossing canvas material cut down on the winds that blew across the deck.

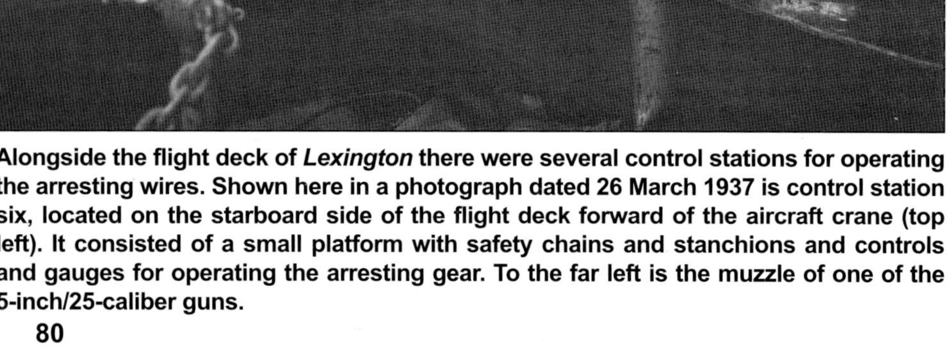

Alongside the flight deck of *Lexington* there were several control stations for operating the arresting wires. Shown here in a photograph dated 26 March 1937 is control station six, located on the starboard side of the flight deck forward of the aircraft crane (top left). It consisted of a small platform with safety chains and stanchions and controls and gauges for operating the arresting gear. To the far left is the muzzle of one of the 5-inch/25-caliber guns.

Control station number four, where arrestor wires numbers five and seven were operated, is viewed on 28 March 1937 with the safety chains and stanchions removed. Mounted on the edge of the flight deck are, left to right, an air-pressure gauge for the yielding elements of the arrestor gear, pneumatic controls for the yielding elements of wires five and seven, pressure-control levers for the two wires, and the yielding element control levers for the wires.

80

At control station number two, shown here, arrestor wires numbers two and four are controlled. The controls and gauge are similar to those depicted in the preceding photograph on page 80, but with a different location for the gauge and the pneumatic control levers.

Landing signal officer Lt. R. S. Clark and his talker are on the LSO's platform behind the windscreen along the flight deck. Using his paddles, the LSO signaled approaching pilots if they were flying too high, too low, too fast, or too slow for a safe, uneventful landing.

Great Lakes BG-1 BuNo 9505 of VB-3B takes off from USS *Lexington* on 23 May 1937. This dive-bomber, of which only 60 were built, was powered by a Pratt & Whitney R-1535-82 radial engine and could carry a 1,000-pound bomb under the fuselage.

On 20 May 1937 a Great Lakes BG-1 has just taken off from the *Lexington* during fleet maneuvers off Hawaii. The BG-1 would have a short tenure on the *Lexington* and would be replaced by the following year with the Vought SB2U-1 Vindicator dive-bomber.

Several Boeing F4B-4s are parked "tailed" up to the smokestack on the USS *Lexington* on 8 May 1937. At the center of the photo, the diagonal port leg of the foremast is visible. To the far left, parts of the gun houses of the twin 8-inch gun turrets are in view.

A Martin M130 flying boat passes over the bow of USS *Lexington* off Hawaii on 19 May 1937. Grumman F2F-1s of VF-2B "Flying Chiefs" are lined up on the forward end of the flight deck. This squadron had been the first to transition to the Grumman F2F-1.

Vought SBU-1 Corsair BuNo 9760 served with VS-3B on the *Lexington* in 1937. The SBU-1 had a maximum speed of 205 miles per hour, a range of 477 miles, and armament of two fixed and one flex-mounted .30-caliber machine guns and 500 pounds of bombs.

The *Lexington* was participating in small-scale war games in company with USS *Saratoga* and USS *Ranger* (CV-4) when photographed on 16 February 1938. The carrier wears a large letter E on the smokestack in honor of winning the annual fleet-wide competition for engineering excellence. From this angle, the absence of the radio-compass booth below the 8-inch control compartment, which was removed in 1935, is apparent.

USS *Lexington* was photographed from USS *Ranger* in March 1938. That month these ships participated in the annual war games, Fleet Problem XIX. The purpose of that year's fleet problem was to test the defenses of both Hawaii and San Francisco. By this time, the U.S. Navy considered a war with Japan to be a very likely possibility, and the annual fleet problems were designed to test the Navy's offensive and defensive theories and prepare the fleet for the most likely scenarios should war come.

In March 1938 during Fleet Problem XIX the USS *Lexington* is anchored off Honolulu, with Diamond Head visible in the distance. During this exercise, the air groups from *Lexington* and *Saratoga* successfully "attacked" Pearl Harbor and, later, San Francisco.

Lexington displays the E award for engineering excellence on her smokestack around 1938. Visible at the base of the smokestack and to its immediate front are three barges; three other boats are on davits amidships, and one appears to be in the boat pocket. (U.S. Naval Shipbuilding Museum)

Around 1939 the *Lexington* is conducting aircraft recovery operations. An airplane is coming in for a landing, and planes that have landed are being grouped to the front of the flight deck. Carrier-based aircraft at this date were still preponderantly biplanes.

In February 1939 the *Lexington* returned to the Caribbean for Fleet Problem XX, a simulation of the defense of the East Coast of the United States. President Roosevelt observed the maneuvers. Here, *Lexington* is at anchor at Guantánamo Bay, Cuba.

A U.S. Navy poster released in November 1939 includes scenes of life in the Navy and, to the lower left of the sailor at the center, a view of USS *Lexington*. The poster appealed to recruits' desire to gain free education, travel to exotic locales, and learn a trade.

Lexington is viewed from above in another photo taken around 1939. The light-colored aircraft contrast strongly with the carrier's flight deck. Once the United States went to war, efforts would be made to match the colors of the flight deck and the aircraft.

The Navy Yard, Puget Sound, at Bremerton, Washington, was a busy yard in the 1930s and would become much busier once the United States entered World War II. It was a key base for the refitting and repair of Navy ships. Even when this photo was taken in 1940, it was a beehive of activity, with numerous ships moored to docks and sitting in dry docks. One of those ships is USS *Lexington*, toward the bottom of the photograph. (National Archives San Bruno via Tracy White)

Following a visit to San Francisco Bay in 1940, USS *Lexington* passes under the Golden Gate Bridge on its way to the ocean. Her air group would land on her after the carrier cleared the Golden Gate. "LEX" is still painted on the aft end of the flight deck. (National Archives San Bruno via Tracy White)

Grumman F2F-1 BuNo 9675 appears in markings for VF-2 "Flying Chiefs" serving on USS *Lexington* in early 1940. The F2F-1 had a maximum speed of 231 miles per hour, range of 750 miles, and armament of two .30-caliber machine guns.

Vought SB2U-2 BuNo 0746 was the aircraft of the commander of VB-2 on the *Lexington* in 1939. The SB2U-2 had a maximum speed of 252, range of 1,002 miles, and armament of one fixed and one flex-mounted .50-caliber machine gun and 1,000 pounds of bombs.

The commander of VT-2 flew this Douglas TBD-1 Devastator in 1938. It had maximum speed of 206 miles per hour, range of 700 miles, and carried one fixed .30- or .50-caliber machine gun, one flex .30-caliber, and a Mk. XIII torpedo or 1,200 pounds of bombs.

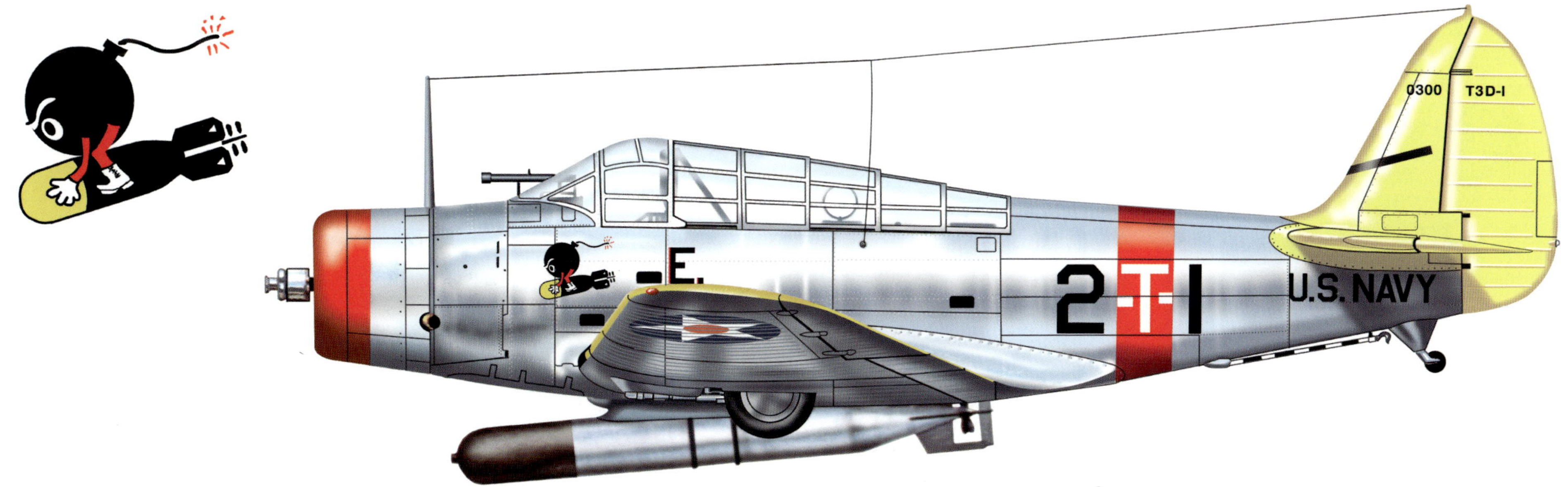

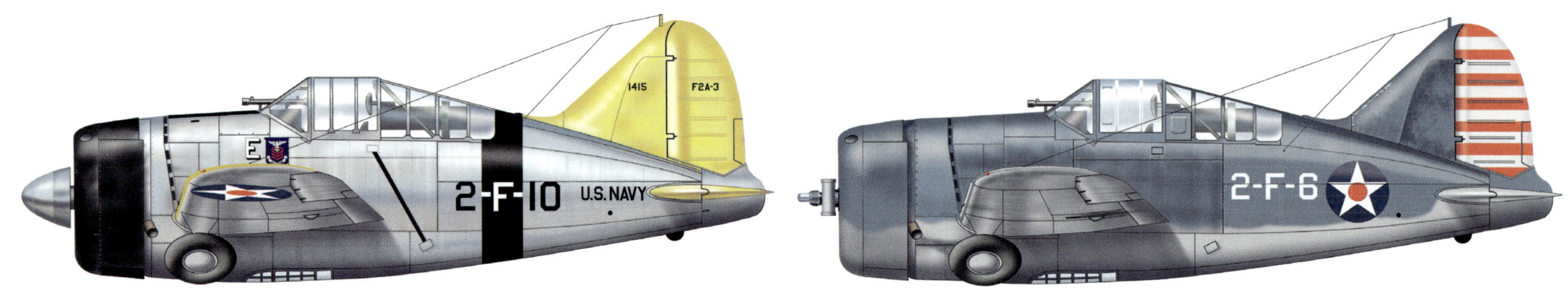

The Brewster F2A Buffalo was intended to replace the Grumman F3F biplane fighter in U.S. Navy service. Despite its ungainly barrel-shaped fuselage, this monoplane presented a more modern appearance than the F3F. Brewster F2A-2 BuNo 1415, shown here, served with VF-2 on *Lexington* in spring 1941. It had an overall Aluminum finish, with black cowl and fuselage rings signifying the leader of the 4th Section of the squadron. The tail color, Lemon Yellow, was that of the *Lexington's* air group. The F2A-2's 1,200-horsepower Wright R-1820-40 radial engine gave the plane a maximum speed of 344 miles per hour. The F2A-2 had a range of 1,670 miles and mounted four fixed .50-caliber machine guns and provisions for two 100-pound bombs. Only 43 F2A-2s were delivered.

A Brewster F2A-3 of VF-2 appears in a camouflage scheme of Nonspecular Blue Gray over Light Gray from January 1942. The final version of the Brewster Buffalo to be produced, the F2A-3, had armament similar to that on the F2A-2. Although the U.S. Navy ordered a total of 108 F2A-3s, the aircraft was already becoming obsolete by the time the order was placed in January 1941. The F2A-3 had a maximum speed of 323 miles per hour and a maximum range of 965 miles. With the addition of fuel tanks in the wings, it boasted greater fuel capacity than the F2A-2, lending the F2A-3 to long-range reconnaissance missions when necessary. The increased fuel capacity and the addition of armor for the pilot also made this a much heavier aircraft, further compromising its performance and usefulness as a fighter.

The *Lexington* in October 1941 had a camouflage scheme of a combination of Measure 1, 5-D Dark Gray on vertical surfaces up to the top of the funnel, and 5-L Light Gray above that level, and Measure 5, which entailed a white false wave painted on each side of the bow.

Lexington steams off San Diego in October 1941. She is painted in the combination of Measures 1 and 5, with the false bow wave prominent. The purpose of this false wave was to give the enemy a false idea of the ship's actual speed, which usually was necessary in their targeting calculations. The Navy had paint problems with the initial lots of 5-D Dark Gray. In an effort to save money, the early production paint was made by adding black to the pre-war gray until it matched 5-D. This practice, however, made the paint less stable and produced chalking and adhesion problems. In this photo, much of *Lexington's* 5-D on the hull appears to have worn off. The island and lower stack maintain the look of fresh 5-D. Later in October the ship was repainted in Measure 12, a graded scheme with Sea Blue up to the level of the hangar deck and Ocean Gray from there to the top of the superstructure.

An aerial view of Ford Island was taken by the U.S. Navy during a November 1941 photographic survey of Pearl Harbor. Moored to the lower right is USS *Lexington*; although this side of Ford Island was where the aircraft carriers moored when in the harbor, *Lexington* was the only carrier present on that date. On Ford Island was Naval Air Station Ford Island. On 7 December 1941, *Lexington* was at sea, and thus escaped the fate of the ships on Battleship Row to the upper left.

At the end of March 1942, the *Lexington*'s four 8-inch gun turrets were removed from the ship to make way for a battery of 1.1-inch automatic antiaircraft guns. In this photograph of that operation, turret number one is hovering over the already removed turret two, suspended from the massive hammerhead crane at Pearl Harbor. The dock holding the crane was specially reinforced for the occasion, and similarly reinforced barges were used to transport the turrets once removed. (Naval History and Heritage Command)

Turret number three is being hoisted from its mounting on 30 March 1942. Details of the doors are visible at the bottom of the photo. These doors are of Dutch-door construction, whereby the entire door or just the upper half could be opened as required. (Naval History and Heritage Command)

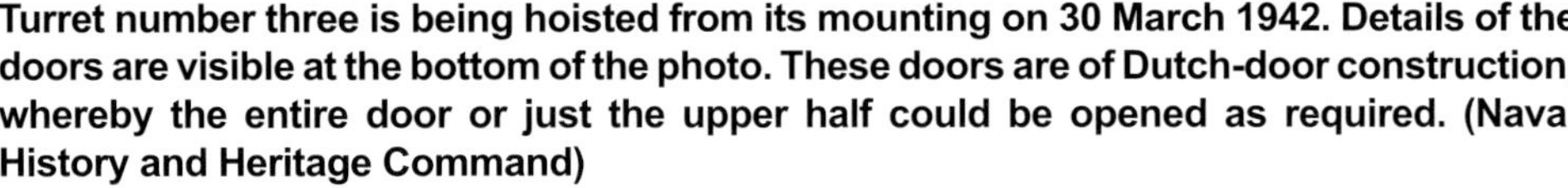

With hoist lines slung under the gun barrels and attached to the gun house, turret three has been landed on a barge next to the *Lexington*. A Japanese invasion of Oahu was still considered a possibility, and the Army needed them for its coastal defenses. (Naval History and Heritage Command)

Turret three is suspended in air and will soon be deposited on a barge lying next to the *Lexington*. Projecting from the upper rear of the gun house of the turret is the left hood of the rangefinder, which was used when the gun mount was under local control. (Naval History and Heritage Command)

With the *Lexington* looming in the background, turrets one and two sit on a dock, and in front of them, two barbette foundation stools rest on a barge in the foreground. The gun house of one of the turrets is hidden behind the barbette foundation stool to the right. (Naval History and Heritage Command)

On 30 March 1942, rigging is in place for hoisting turret number three clear of its mounting aft of the smokestack. Care was taken to avoid hitting the 8-inch fire-control station above the gun house of the turret. Anti-splinter matting has been installed on the sides of the 8-inch fire-control station as well as on the 5-inch fire-control station above it. Toward the rear of the machine gun platform near the top of the smokestack is a 36-inch searchlight. (Naval History and Heritage Command)

Although one of the primary Japanese objectives in striking Pearl Harbor on 7 December 1941 was the decimation of the U.S. carrier force, none of the American floating aerodromes was present that morning.

Lexington had sailed from Pearl two days before, bound for Midway, transporting Marine Scout Bomber Squadron 231 to that island, where it was envisioned the Marine aviators would bolster the defenses. *Lexington* was 425 miles from her destination when word of the Japanese surprise attack reached the small task force. Immediately a search for the Japanese fleet was begun, to no avail, and *Lexington* and her Task Force 12 then rendezvoused with *Enterprise's* Task Force 8, continuing the search until all returned to a devastated Pearl Harbor on 13 December.

The next day *Lexington* sailed again, headed first toward Jaluit in the Marshall Islands, and then redirected toward Wake. However, Wake fell before *Lexington* and the other carriers, *Saratoga* and *Enterprise,* could reach the island. *Lexington* turned course and returned to Pearl Harbor on 27 December.

Lexington and her crew conducted relatively routine operations until 20 February 1942, the routine only being interrupted by the launching of an attack on a suspected Japanese submarine on 10 January, and the sinking of *Lexington's* supporting fleet oiler, *Neches,* on 23 January.

On 20 February 1942, while moving against Japanese forces on Rabaul, *Lexington* was attacked by two waves of Japanese 4th Air Group Mitsubishi G4M "Betty" bombers. Nine bombers in the first wave and eight in the second wave pounced on Lex. *Lexington's* antiaircraft batteries opened up, and according to initial belief, brought down some of the attackers. Later analysis, however, credited *Lexington's* Combat Air Patrol with truly saving the day, downing 16 of the 17 attacking Japanese planes. More remarkably, Lt. Edward "Butch" O'Hare, flying an F4F Wildcat, downed five of the bombers that were intent on sinking *Lexington.* The feat not only earned O'Hare the title of "ace," it also won him the Medal of Honor.

After 54 days in the combat zone, including a 10 March attack on New Guinea, *Lexington* returned to Pearl Harbor on 26 March. There she was repaired, and major modifications were begun to her defenses. One of the most visible changes made to the ship was the removal of her four two-gun 8-inch/55-caliber turrets in preparation for the installation of four new dual-purpose 5-inch, 38-caliber twin mounts, which would have substantially bolstered the carrier's antiaircraft defenses. The Japanese attack on Pearl Harbor had proven the unlikelihood of a carrier being involved in a surface action, and the necessity of mounting a powerful antiaircraft battery aboard carriers.

In the event, however, the 5-inch, 38-caliber mounts for *Lexington* were not yet available at Pearl Harbor in early April 1942, and so she put to sea on 15 April with seven 1.1-inch quad mounts installed instead. Meanwhile, her old 8-inch turrets were not discarded; rather, they were given to the Army, which installed them as coastal defense batteries Wilridge and Opaeula in Hawaii, where they remained until scrapped in 1948.

For *Lexington* and her crew, the days after leaving the shipyard in April 1942 were filled with relatively routine work, transporting VMF-211 and their F2A Buffalos, and training operations for the ship's own crew. By the end of the month, however, operations were in motion that would bring *Lexington* to the Coral Sea, and her fate.

The *Lexington* from the stern to the forward end of the superstructure is viewed during the ship's refitting at Pearl Harbor on 31 March 1942. During this refit, the ship received other modifications, including the addition of 22 20mm antiaircraft gun mounts, most of which were installed on four new antiaircraft-gun galleries: one on the starboard side of the base of the smokestack, two in a boat pocket on the port side of the hull, and one in the starboard boat pocket. (Naval History and Heritage Command)

This Grumman F4F-3 of VF-3 was Lt. Cdr. John S. "Jimmy" Thach's plane in spring 1942. It had a maximum speed of 331 miles per hour, range of 845 miles, armament of four wing-mounted .50-caliber machine guns, and could mount two 100-pouund bombs.

The *Lexington*'s 8-inch turrets enjoyed a second life as U.S. Army coastal-defense guns on the island of Oahu. Her sister ship *Saratoga* also transferred its 8-inch turrets to the Army in early 1942. One of the turrets formerly of those carriers is seen to the right. (U.S. Army Museum of Hawaii)

An army corporal stands next to one of the 8-inch turrets from the *Lexington*-class carriers recycled as a coastal-defense gun mount. Those turrets were emplaced at four installations on Oahu: Batteries Burgess, Kirkpatrick, Ricker, and Riggs. (U.S. Army Museum of Hawaii)

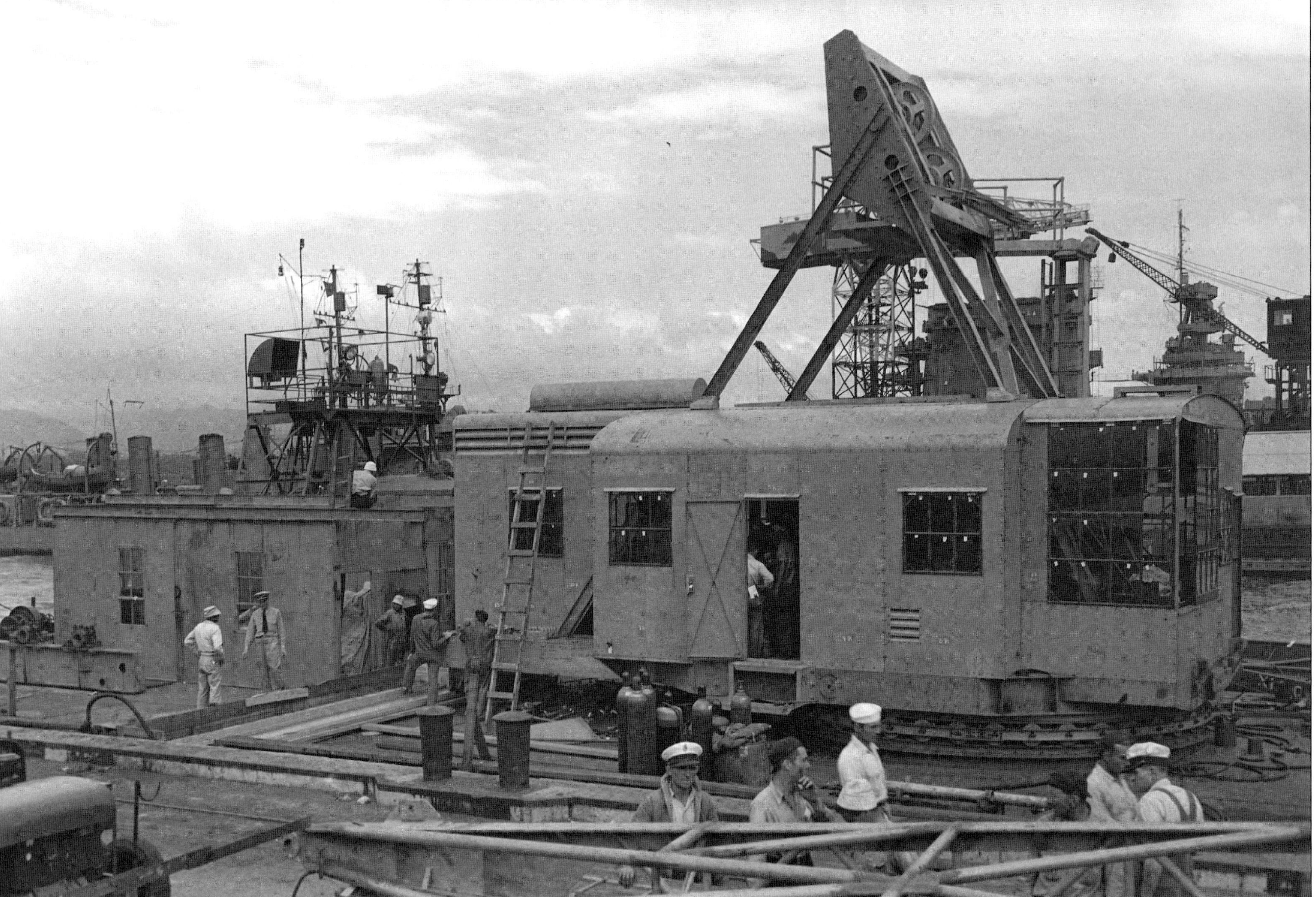

Visible through the shipyard machinery and equipment in the foreground is the USS *Lexington* on 13 April 1942 during her refitting at Pearl Harbor. Several noteworthy details are visible on the ship. Anti-splinter matting is present on the navigation bridge and possibly on higher levels of the superstructure and battery-control stations as well. On the top front of the smokestack are a CXAM-1 "mattress" radar antenna installed in 1941 and a smoke deflector. The flag plot has been extended and the rangefinder moved from the top of the pilothouse to the top of the flag plot. (National Archives via James Noblin)

This Douglas SBD-3 served with VS-2 in May 1942. The SBD-3 had a maximum speed of 250 miles per hour, range of 1,560 miles, and was armed with two fixed .50-caliber machine guns, one or two flex .30-caliber machine guns, and 1,600 pounds in bombs.

Two legendary pilots, Jimmy Thach, foreground, and Edward H. "Butch" O'Hare, of VF-3, fly their Grumman Wildcats in April 1942. O'Hare was awarded the Medal of Honor for shooting down five Japanese planes attacking the *Lexington* on 20 February 1942. (Naval History and Heritage Command)

Acting on orders from Admiral Nimitz, *Lexington,* along with *Yorktown* and escorting vessels, were sent into the Coral Sea to defend Tulagi and Port Moresby. There, *Lexington* would take part in the U.S. Navy's first carrier-vs.-carrier combat action. At 0815 hours on 7 May what was believed to be the main Japanese force was spotted just 175 miles north of *Lexington.* An hour and 11 minutes later, *Lexington* launched her attack aircraft, with *Yorktown* following suit a half hour later. At about 1100 hours, *Lexington's* attack aircraft spotted the Japanese carrier *Shōhō* and attacked, with *Yorktown's* joining in when they arrived. In all, 93 U.S. Navy aircraft savaged the Japanese ship. An estimated seven torpedoes and 13 1,000-pound bombs found their marks, sending *Shōhō* beneath the waves just 36 minutes after the first strike.

But *Shōhō* was not alone, and at 1630, the carriers *Shōkaku* and *Zuikaku* launched their aircraft to avenge the loss of the *Shōhō.* The 12 dive bombers and 15 torpedo bombers failed to find the U.S. vessels, but were themselves attacked by the American Combat Air Patrol, which downed nine Japanese bombers at the cost of two U.S. fighters. As the sun sank lower in the sky, some of the surviving Japanese spotted the American carriers, but rather than attacking, mistook them for their own and attempted to land, an effort that ended in their destruction.

At dawn the next day, *Lexington's* aircraft began hunting for the Japanese carriers, hoping to replicate the previous day's successes. Presently, the Japanese carriers were located, and at 0915 both *Lexington* and *Yorktown* attacked. The results were not as good as the day before, with *Shōkaku* only receiving moderate damage. Worse, the returning U.S. aircraft were trailed by the Japanese, who pinpointed the location of both *Lexington* and *Yorktown* and launched their own strike force of 90 planes. Eight torpedoes were launched at *Yorktown,* but through superb seamanship she avoided all of them. The considerably greater size of *Lexington,* however, made her a bigger target, and less responsive. She was struck by two of the 11 torpedoes the Japanese hurled at her. Then two of the Japanese dive bombers scored hits on *Lexington.* Despite these damages, the ship's strength and the valiant efforts of her damage control parties kept *Lexington* in fighting form for an hour and 15 minutes after her last attacker left. Then, however, gasoline vapors ignited and the resultant fire and explosion doomed the ship.

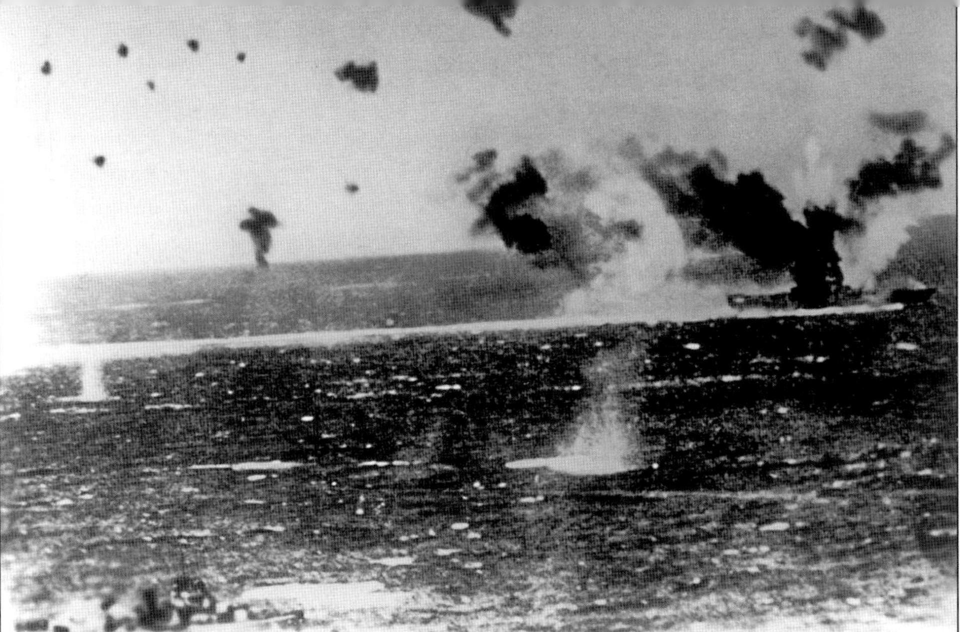

On 15 April 1942, *Lexington* left Pearl Harbor with Task Force 11 bound for the South Pacific. This force clashed with the Imperial Japanese Navy in the Battle of the Coral Sea. In this photo, *Lexington* is viewed from USS *Yorktown* (CV-5) during the battle. (Naval History and Heritage Command)

At about 11:05 on the morning of 8 May 1942 in the Battle of the Coral Sea, Japanese aircraft located the *Lexington* and soon commenced an attack on her. At 11:20 they scored two torpedo hits on port side of the carrier. In this photo, explosions wrack the ship. (Naval History and Heritage Command)

In this photograph, *Lexington* is under attack by Japanese dive-bombers on 8 May and is maneuvering in an attempt to dodge the bombs. Two bombs struck the ship, one killing the crew of a 5-inch antiaircraft gun and starting fires, and another hitting the smokestack. (Naval History and Heritage Command)

On the day before the *Lexington* came under attack, at 12:00 on 7 May, her air group, commanded by Cdr. William B. Ault, struck a hard blow, hitting the carrier IJN *Shōhō* with two 1,000-pound bombs and five torpedoes. After more attacks, *Shōhō* sank. (San Diego Air and Space Museum)

Following the Japanese attack on *Lexington*, emergency crews put out the fires on deck, and the carrier was able to recover its air group, returning from attacks on the Japanese fleet, that afternoon. A crewman surveys damage to the forward port 5-inch gun gallery. (Naval History and Heritage Command)

In a view taken from next to the island facing forward around 1700 hours on 8 May 1942, crewmen of the *Lexington* prepare to abandon ship. That order would be issued at 17:07, when all surviving crewmen, around 2,770 in all, would be evacuated to other ships. (Naval History and Heritage Command)

Two crewmen survey the damage to 5-inch mount number six at the aft end of the forward port gallery. The damage to the gun gallery was caused by a bomb that pierced the deck just beyond these men and exploded in an ammunition locker one deck below. (Naval History and Heritage Command)

Damage to the forward port 5-inch guns is shown. Three men of the crew of 5-inch gun mount number four, the one pointing outboard, were killed by the bomb blast. A second bomb that hit the ship struck on the port side of the smokestack, killing some crewmen. (National Archives via Rob Stern)

The forward port 5-inch gun gallery is viewed from its forward end facing aft in the aftermath of the attack. In the foreground is 5-inch mount number two, with mount four just aft of it. *Lexington*'s preliminary combat report listed no damage to mount two. (National Archives via Rob Stern)

In the foreground, facing aft, is 5-inch mount number four in the forward port gallery. Next to the mount is a crewman wearing a life jacket, apparently surveying the damage. The bomb that caused this damage is thought to have weighed less than 200 pounds. (National Archives via Rob Stern)

Following a series of internal explosions and fires on the afternoon of 8 May, *Lexington*'s power plant was shut down at 16:30, and at 17:07 Capt. Frederick Sherman gave the order to abandon ship. In this photo, crewmen are lowering themselves by lines into the water. (U.S. Naval Shipbuilding Museum)

The abandoning of *Lexington* was well documented in numerous photographs. In this one, crewmen are using knotted lines to hoist themselves up onto one of the *Lexington*'s escort ships, which did heroic service fighting fires on the carrier and rescuing its crew. (San Diego Air and Space Museum)

At 17:27 on 8 May 1942, a large internal explosion amidships, thought to have been caused by the detonation of torpedo warheads, blew off the aft elevator and hurled aircraft into the air. This photograph shows that catastrophic explosion. (Naval History and Heritage Command)

The massive explosion set off by the detonation of ordnance at 17:27 is viewed a moment after the preceding photograph was taken. The escort ships had backed away from the carrier by then. More of the *Lexington*'s crewmen were killed in the explosion. (U.S. Navy)

Following the massive explosion, the *Lexington* is a seething mass of destruction amidships. Amazingly, aircraft are still present at the rear of the flight deck. Many crewmen were still on the carrier at this time, attempting to get off the ship. (U.S. Navy)

After a series of explosions wracked *Lexington* in the late afternoon of 8 May, the destroyer USS *Phelps* (DD-360) was ordered to sink the mortally wounded carrier. *Phelps* sent three torpedoes into *Lexington*, and the ship went below the waves at 19:56.

The sinking of USS *Lexington* marked another in a series of dark days for the United States and its Navy following the 7 December 1941 attack on Pearl Harbor. In spring 1942 the U.S. Navy had only a handful of carriers in the Pacific and could ill afford to lose one. Although 26 officers and 190 crewmen of the *Lexington* were lost on 8 May 1942, the balance of her crew, 2,735 in all, was saved, and these officers and men, with the benefit of battle experience, would go on to staff the carriers that soon would flow from America's shipyards to the battle fronts. Lady Lex, as she was affectionately called by her crew, helped hold the line against Japanese expansion in the South Pacific in those perilous first months of the war, and she would stand as a powerful symbol of American resolve. (San Diego Air and Space Museum)